I0062140

Crypto Scams

How to Avoid Bitcoin and Cryptocurrency Scams

(Non Technical Steps in Detecting Crypto Rugpulls and Potential Scam Tokens)

Michael Toland

Published By **Andrew Zen**

Michael Toland

All Rights Reserved

Crypto Scams: How to Avoid Bitcoin and Cryptocurrency Scams (Non Technical Steps in Detecting Crypto Rugpulls and Potential Scam Tokens)

ISBN   978-1-998038-49-7

No part of this guidebook shall be reproduced in any form without permission in writing from the publisher except in the case of brief quotations embodied in critical articles or reviews.

Legal & Disclaimer

The information contained in this book is not designed to replace or take the place of any form of medicine or professional medical advice. The information in this book has been provided for educational & entertainment purposes only.

The information contained in this book has been compiled from sources deemed reliable, and it is accurate to the best of the Author's knowledge; however, the Author cannot guarantee its accuracy and validity and cannot be held liable for any errors or omissions. Changes are periodically made to this book. You must consult your doctor or get professional medical advice before using any of the suggested remedies, techniques, or information in this book.

Upon using the information contained in this book, you agree to hold harmless the Author from and against any damages, costs, and expenses, including any legal fees potentially resulting from the application of any of the information provided by this guide. This disclaimer applies to any damages or injury caused by the use and application, whether directly or indirectly, of any advice or information presented, whether for breach of contract, tort, negligence, personal injury, criminal intent, or under any other cause of action.

You agree to accept all risks of using the information presented inside this book. You need to consult a professional medical practitioner in order to ensure you are both able and healthy enough to participate in this program.

Table Of Contents

Chapter 1: How to Spot a Crypto Scam

Certain websites promise massive returns for small cryptocurrency investments. There are fake reviews to appear authentic. They have promise of FOMO and easy to use dashboards which resemble many of the financial websites. Although the language is a bit sloppy, If you're attentive enough, you'll see that the site is not as normal.

One of these sites is Coindeskminers.com. Its website states:

"They say money doesn't grow from the ground, well it does with cryptocurrencies [sic] because at Coindesk Miners we have assembled a group of world-class engineering, strategic cryptocurrency mining and investment logic growing investments and making profits for both parties."

The claims on many websites are easy: Just make a small amount of crypto sometimes as low than $5. Then, are sure to earn instant rewards. Unfortunately, this is all fraud, but nobody will be able to recognize. They usually use techniques to create and upfront fee fraud. Because cryptos aren't refundable in the event that the user chooses to do so and banks are unable to intervene to stop transaction, the fraud begins by causing the victim to lose the money instantly.

All money that you transfer to the scammers will be gone once the scammers present you with the money they made from your funds and demand more cash to cover the 'fees' making the victim pay more money to get the investment as well as fake earnings back. They then vanish with all your cash.

How Crypto Scams Work

In the past, a lot of crypto-investors have been taken with a large amount of actual funds. According to reports, losses from cryptocurrency scams during 2018 reached up around US$1.7 billion. Criminals make use of both the latest technologies and older methods to scam innocent users who are who are transferring money via blockchains.

When you look up crypto, blockchain and cybercrime, one s evident that many of the fraudsters are based on tried-and-true Ponzi strategies that make use of money that new investors deposit for the purpose of paying out dividends to older investors.

However other systems use extremely sophisticated and highly automated processes. There are some that use automated software that works with Telegram. Telegram is an instant messaging platform that is a favorite among most people who are fascinated by cryptocurrency. Although a cryptocurrency scheme is genuine there are criminals that could alter its value in the market.

One question that comes up is how can the innocent users be attracted by crypto-scams?

Fast-Talking Swindlers

Certain criminals target the investors' lust for money, offering massive profits. As an example, unidentified individuals operate the scam bot iCenter which is which is a Ponzi scheme that targets Bitcoin as well as Litecoin. The site does not provide any information about investments, however it claims 1.2 percent daily return. The iCenter runs on an online Telegram Group Chat.

It starts with a small group of fraudsters who are involved in the scam and they are given a referral number to share with their friends via social media as well as on blogs. The intention is to convince victims who are not aware to join in the conversation. After that, newcomers receive enthralling and thrilling messages from scammers who were the first to contact them.

A few newcomers might choose to invest, and at time, scammers give them a unique bitcoin wallet in which they could put the bitcoins. The scammers then convince them to hold off for possibly between 99 and 120 days in order to earn massive gains.

In the time between waiting and getting their money on the other hand, unaware victims typically make use of social media to pass on referral code with their friends and acquaintances. This brings more people to the group chat, and then instantly into the investment plan.

There is no investment in the money that can be made in any legal firm. When new employees are recruited, the person who recruited them is awarded an amount of new money and the cycle repeats.

They distribute the old participants in each session of investors who are younger. A few members are determined to raise new money. They also post instructional videos as well as photos of themselves with massive amounts of cash as an incentive to sign up for the fraud.

Convincing Lies

Certain crypto frauds make use of deceit straight out of the box. As an example, the creators of the Onecoin scam cryptocurrency stole up approximately $3.8 billion in funds from their investors convincing investors that their nonexistent crypto currency was actually real.

The other scams are built on attracting potential victims by presenting claims and the jargons of experts. Global Trading scammers Global Trading scammers allegedly exploited the prices of the various exchanges to benefit by gaining arbitrage. This is the practice of buying at a low price and then selling for higher price. It's like they took the money of investors.

Global Trading successfully used a bot to use Telegram also. The victims would be able to send an inquiry regarding balance. They were provided with inaccurate information about their accounts balances, and sometimes they'd see their balances grow by as much as 1% within just an hour. In the wake of such impressive returns, users were lured to spread the news with friends and relatives.

Exploiting Friends and Family

When a scam is initiated the scheme is alive for a time, most notably via social media. People who aren't aware of the scam get lured with promises of huge gains from crypto investment. They spread the information to their friends and family members and then the fraudster takes on more victims.

There are times when prominent names may be involved in these scams. One example is that a thief who was behind GainBitcoin and a variety of scams across India was able to get numerous Bollywood celebrities to endorse his book "Cryptocurrency for Beginners." The author tried to become a household name as a "cryptocurrency guru. He was the leader of efforts to cost investors between $769-$2 billion.

Chapter 2: Fake Initial Coin Offerings

The initial coin offering method was once a well-known scam that led to China prohibit ICO in its territory. An investment possibility that could be legitimate and an ICO obviously is a method for an emerging crypto company to get funds from prospective customers. Investors can expect a discounted rate on new cryptocoins, to send cryptocurrency that is active, such as ethereum or bitcoin.

The majority of ICOs proved to be a scam, with participants engaging in shady plans, including leasing fake offices and creating fancy promotional documents. The media's publicity about cryptos sparked an influx of ICO frauds in the year 2017. One year later, more than 1,000 ICO initiatives failed, costing the investors over $100 million.

The majority of these projects did not have innovative ideas, with greater than 15% copying previous cryptocurrency initiatives. Even the supporting documentation was copied. Investors looking for returns from a rapidly developing technology sector remain attracted by cryptocurrency and blockchains. But, they're somewhat new even to the sellers. Therefore, novices and experts are also a victim of frauds involving crypto.

With the emerging crypto market in which everything is susceptible to change the investors should be very cautious. Make sure to conduct thorough investigations into the background of any projects which you are planning to invest in so that you can be sure whether they're legitimate and are not a gang of criminals looking to take advantage of others.

Imposter Websites

You could be taking a valid advice by a person with a lot of knowledge, yet fall into the hands of criminals when going to a fake website. A lot of websites have been designed to look like legitimate startup businesses. If you don't see an icon of a lock that signifies security in the URL bar but not a single 'https' on the address of your website, you should take care.

Although the website may appear to appear identical with the one you were hoping to go to You may get redirected to a different website for making payments. In the case of a payment, say you click on a legit hyperlink, but

Hackers have made a false URL that contains zero rather than the letter "o". The platform does not lead you to a crypto investment you've researched previously.

To prevent these issues To avoid this, be sure to type the URL exactly into your browser, and then be sure to check it thoroughly.

Phony Mobile Apps

The scammers can also fool cryptocurrency investors with fake applications which are free to download through Google Play and the Apple App Store. Although the authorities are able to identify these apps are fake and they get the apps removed, that doesn't mean fake apps aren't negatively impacting many financial accounts. Numerous unsuspecting users have downloaded bogus crypto applications.

Even though it may be a risky option for Android users, every investor must be alert to the potential. Check for obvious misspellings within the description and, sometimes the application's name. It could also appear fake with weird coloring or wrong logos. If you notice some of these characteristics be sure to stay clear of the application.

Social Media Updates

If you follow celebrities as well as executives on social media There is a chance that you're following impostor accounts. Similar situations apply to crypto currencies, in which case fraudulent and impersonating bots are often seen. Stay away from offers that come via social media, particularly Facebook and Twitter specifically where the end result can be difficult to verify. There are fake accounts everywhere.

If anyone on these platforms asks for the smallest amount of your bitcoin the chances are high that you'll never receive the money returned. It is important to be vigilant even if other users are responding to the request. It is possible that they could be bots or other criminals who are associated with the scheme.

Scamming Emails

In the event that you get an email that is similar to the one you received from a legitimate crypto firm take care to stay clear of being enticed by. Verify that the email address is identical and the logo or brand is the same. Find out if it's possible to verify that this email address is linked to the organization you're looking to.

Ability to scrutinize every detail is just one reason why you should choose to work with firms with real employees employed by their clients. If you are unsure concerning an email, speak to anyone who is employed by the organization. Beware of clicking a link within any email to go on a web page.

In the ICO boom, fraudsters often made announcements of fake projects in means of taking large sums of money. Investors should stay clear of these fake emails and web-based advertisements. Be sure to read every detail before putting funds into any endeavor.

There are numerous loopholes in which Internet users use unsecure computing systems to mine or take cryptocurrency. Be sure your computers are secured and secure within this rapidly growing market.

Cryptojacking

Criminals are profiting from the emerging cryptocurrency industry to extort unsuspecting customers. They employ ransomware-like methods and smuggled websites to gain access to the computers of employees to be used for mining cryptocurrency.

As described, crypto-jacking often referred to criminal crypto mining, is a rising online risk that is able to hide on computers as well as a mobile. The machine's resources are used to mine different kinds of digital money, also known as crypto-currencies.

Cyber-hackers could hijack a web browser while simultaneously compromising any device, from desktops and laptops to phones, to server networks.

Like many various other shady attacks against computer users it is driven by earnings. But, unlike other attacks, cryptojacking has been specifically designed to be completely hidden from the users.

Hackers are able to hack cryptographic codes by causing the user to click the malicious link in an email. The malicious program then runs cryptomining codes on the user's device. Cybercriminals may also attack websites or an advertising on the web by introducing JavaScript script that runs automatically when it has been loaded into the browser of the victim.

The cryptomining program runs behind the scenes while unaware victims run their PCs regularly. The only indication they could notice is slower performance or delays in the execution.

Instead of constructing a dedicated cryptomining machine, cybercriminals employ the strategy of cryptojacking to steal computer resources from victim's devices. Once all the resources have been put together, hackers will be able to take on complex cryptomining activities without incurring significant costs.

The majority of victims of cryptojacking do not know that their networks or devices are infected. This software was designed to hide from person using it, yet it exacts its toll on network and devices. The stealing of resources raises costs for electricity and reduces the useful life of the device.

Chapter 3: How Cryptojacking Works

The cryptojackers are able to enslave devices by using a variety of methods. A method used by them is similar to the typical malware. The victims are enticed to click an unintentional link within an email. It then loads cryptocurrency mining code right onto the computer. When the device is infected, hackers start doing all day long mining crypto, as they hide in the darkness.

As it's the computer system, it can be classified as a local, persistent danger that has infected the system itself. Another method for cryptojacking is sometimes referred to as drive-by cryptocurrency mining. Similar to the shady advertisement attacks the method involves embedding a bit of JavaScript code within a Web page. When it is done code, it executes crypto mining on the computers of users which visit the page infected.

"Drive-by cryptomining can even infect your Android mobile device."

At the beginning of crypto mining by drive-by, websites that were caught in the cryptocurrency craze sought to increase their revenues and increase the value of their website traffic. They had openly asked the permission of visitors to mine cryptos they were on their site. Then they offered it up as an exchange fair to all in which you are granted free content when the site administrator makes use of your computer to do mining.

If someone is visiting an online gaming website, they will probably stay at the site for a certain duration as the JavaScript software mines coins. After which, when a user leaves the website, the cryptomining process also ceases, and frees the computer.

It is theoretically an unwise idea so in the event that the website is honest and transparent regarding their actions. But, it's difficult in the real world to judge if the website is operating in a fair manner.

The most malicious variants of the drive-by cryptomining don't need consent from the user. It even continues to operate long even after users leave the original website. It's a standard method used by the owners of fake websites, and even by hackers that have hacked legitimate websites.

The majority of users do not realize of the fact that the website they visit was using their computer to mine cryptocurrency. This code makes use of the system resources and must remain undetected. While the user believes all browsers are shut, a hidden one stays active. It is usually an pop-under which is designed so that it can be hidden beneath the taskbar, or just behind a clock.

Drive-by cryptomining may even infect Android mobile devices. It operates in the same strategy that is used to attack desktops. Certain attacks could occur through the use of a Trojan disguised inside the downloaded app.also there is the possibility that user's smartphones could be taken to a malicious website that generates a constant pop-under.

Incredibly, there's an Trojan available recognized for its ability to penetrate Android phones by installing an application that's quite malicious. The program can actually take the processor out of your device until the point that it overheats and causes the battery to bulge. This malware renders your Android in a state of death following a prolonged use.

It is possible to ask, "Why use my phone and its relatively minor processing power?" But in the event that these hacks are carried out in a masse, the greater number of phones accessible adds to a collective power that warrants cybercriminals pay attention.

A few cybersecurity experts claim that in contrast to other forms of malware, cryptojacking software does have no risk of causing harm to computer systems or' personal information. However, the stealing of CPU resources comes with its own effects.

This can result in slow computer performance that could make it difficult for the user.

In the case of larger companies that could have been affected by multiple schemes of cryptojacking there are real expenses. The cost of IT staff, the electricity costs and wasted opportunities are just a few effects of when an enterprise is targeted with drive-by cryptojacking.

How Common Is Cryptojacking?

Cryptojacking is quite new. It is however growing to be one of the biggest cyber-attacks as per cybersecurity experts. Since the last 3 years, we have seen an increase in cases of hackers attempting to hack into users across all over the world. In October of 2017, Fortune stated that cryptojacking would be the next security issue that could affect users across the world.

In the initial quarter of 2018 there was a 4000% rise in the detects of malware that is based on Android. Additionally, cryptojackers continue to develop their techniques through ad hoc attacks on increasingly robust hardware.

In one instance, one instance in which hackers stole the operating technology network which is part of an European utilities control systems. They managed to compromise the ability of operators to control the facility. Another incident from the same article, some Russian scientists in an organization allegedly utilized the supercomputer in the nuclear warhead and research facility to create Bitcoin.

"Criminals even seem to prefer cryptojacking to ransomware."

Although these breaches are as shocking as they may seem, hacking personal devices with cryptojacking remains one of the biggest issues. Cybercriminals prefer this technique as stealing small amounts from multiple devices could produce large amounts of money that do not draw the attention of authorities or security teams.

Incredibly, criminals are now appearing to favor cryptojacking over ransomware which relies upon cryptocurrency for ransom payment that is anonymous. Cryptojacking may pay hackers a higher sum for lower dangers compared to ransomware.

Chapter 4: How To Avoid Falling Victim To Cryptojacking

If you're a victim of cryptojacking local to your device, or via the web browser, it could be extremely difficult to spot the intrusion on your own. This is done to shield away from your. Additionally, finding out the cause of the excessive CPU use could be a bit difficult. These processes could be concealing their own activities or disguised in a legitimate way to stop your ability to stop the abuse.

In addition to criminals on the internet, if your device is operating at full capacity, it's going to perform extremely slowly. It becomes difficult to solve the issue. Similar to similar to other security measures against malware It is highly recommended to set up security prior to fall victim to cyber-criminals.

One solution is to block JavaScript from the browser you use for all your browsing on the internet. Although it does not stop the drive-by cryptojacking process, it could hinder the use of various features that you might enjoy and want.

Other specialized software is also available, such as "MinerBlock" and "No Coin', which stop every mining activity in the most the most popular browsers. They both come with extensions available for Firefox, Chrome, and Opera. It's interesting to note that Opera's most recent versions come with NoCoin integrated.

"Whether attackers try to use malware, a browser-based drive-by download, or a Trojan, you're protected against cryptojacking."

However, experts advise that it is better to avoid an ad-hoc program, instead opt for a greater security software. Like, Malwarebytes protects users from far more than simply the threat of cryptojacking. It also blocks malware, ransomware, as well as other threats on the internet. If cybercriminals attempt to make use of a drive-by download that is based on a browser malware, malware, or Trojan (like Emotet), you'll be completely secure from cyber-attacks that involve cryptojacking.

In an environment of cyber threats which is always changing keeping your computer safe from most recent threats like cyber-cyptojacking is an all-hours job. By using the most effective and sophisticated tools, you'll be able to find and remove any kind of attack and ensure that the computer's resources are secure.

Pump And Dump

A "pump-and dump" scheme is a unique form of financial fraud which has been known to increase the cost of a currency through propagation of false information. While this type of scam isn't recent, it has seen an enormous resurgence in the world of cryptocurrency. Studies that were published in Crime Science utilized the computational method to find those schemes needed to be used in any future massive-scale surveillance investigation.

The 1700s were the time when some insiders employed by the British-based South Sea Company started spreading outrageous claims regarding the achievements and future of the company as a giant trading firm within South America.

Although they knew that the company was unlikely to make any revenue, they were able to lure investors in the wrong direction and elevated the cost of its shares to new heights prior to its collapse that shook the whole British economy.

It was among the earliest recorded instances of a "pump-and-dump" scheme': a form of fraud committed by insiders, who manipulate prices of commodities through spreading false information.

While this kind of manipulative scheme is not new, the method remains in use until today. The pump-and-dump scheme has been described as a kind of microcap fraud that involves the use of low-priced penny stocks since they were thought as simpler to manipulate.

Recently, the scam has experienced a revival in the cryptocurrency world which is largely not regulated. Unregulated, this market makes it a tempting opportunity for fraudsters trying to take advantage of people who have no idea.

Pumps and dumps follow a standard pattern that is comprised of three major steps. The accumulation occurs when a criminal purchases a product for a very low cost. This is followed by a pump stage that artificially boosts the demand for the commodity, and therefore the price. In the end, dumping begins after the criminals who have bought through the accumulation phase decide to dispose of their possessions, resulting with a sharp drop in the price.

A model of the pump-and-dump form and its various phases (reproduced by Kamps & Kleinberg, 2018)

Research has shown that the duration for modern pump and dump schemes is reducing. Pumps today reach their peak in minutes or just a few seconds. Interestingly, the majority of crypto-related groups are organized via chat rooms on the internet like Discord as well as Telegram. Crypto scams are publically available to anyone who wants to be a part of it.

The potential for earnings is not certain due to the fact that pumps generally have a limited duration, that makes it difficult to determine the time of highest point. A majority of the time, an organization selects the coin that will be used and announces that the pump will take place at a certain time, without naming the exact date.

Once the moment is right that the coin pump is revealed and people are expected to purchase in the quickest time possible. Members of the criminal group are urged to promote the idea that this coin will be the next thing to be announced. The way they do this is through social media. It is a tactic to entice ignorant investors by exploiting the fear of being left out (FOMO) for the next major investment.

It is an excellent chance for insiders to make use of their knowledge about when a coins are going to be increased to earn profits, as they are able to acquire it prior and sell it at highest price.

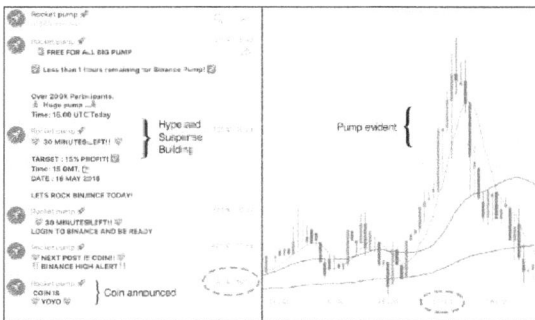

A sample of a crypto pump and dump group (left) with the associated exchange data (right). The data is derived by Kamps as well as Kleinberg (2018)

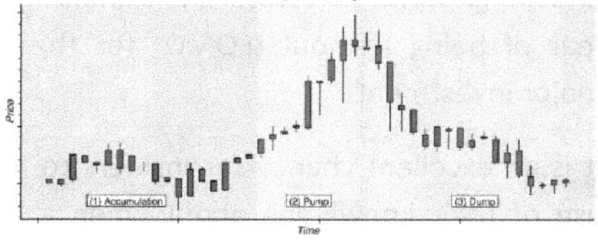

Pump and Dump

(1) Accumulation   (2) Pump   (3) Dump

Time

Chapter 5: Findings Of The Research

Researchers have discovered that the switch towards more real-time strategies through the pump and dump actors have reduced the duration of pumps running for just few seconds or minutes prior to when the maximum is reached. An algorithmic approach was employed to find these types of schemes.

The same strategy is a good idea for the any future work to detect large-scale crypto pumps and dumps since hundreds of markets are available on numerous exchanges. Manually reviewing all of them isn't possible.

Like the classic penny-stock markets Cryptos that are most susceptible to attacks are the ones with less popularity with a significant decrease in market capitalizations. Fraudsters are attracted to them due to the fact that they have a low amount of liquidity, which allows them to be more easily manipulated.

In addition, approximately 30% of cryptocurrency pairs studied represented around 80percent of all reported pump-and dump activity. Through a criminal science approach, scientists try to understand how these frauds work in order to develop the best prevention strategies. The development of a computer-based method to identify these scams and learn from patterns that are observed is one of the most important steps towards prevention's primary goal.

Other than the investors, who knew about the scam with crypto, no one other person is left with an income. The majority of paid or free group for pump and dump were created by the scammers. If you don't understand the group's organizers well There is a good chance that you will get scammed by paid-for groups too.

The majority of stock exchanges and cryptocurrency exchanges come with software to detect crypto frauds. Experts say that if an offer is so good it's impossible to believe the chances are it's untrue. So, you should stay clear of the idea.

How Crypto Pump-And-Dump Scams Operate

Numerous news reports have reported or provided anonymous account of schemes to alter cryptocurrency trading through pump-and-dump scheme. In the words of Journal the Crypto pump-and-dump strategies function like those early days in the world of stock markets. In the past when traders were causing havoc, they smashed the market, manipulating prices through group purchases.

Similar dynamics are utilized within the cryptocurrency space. A few well-coordinated traders generate excitement for cryptocurrency through a series of comments on the benefits through a variety of channels, such as socia media. They create a purchasing frenzy. Its value rises as other dealers not affiliated with the criminal group join the buying spree, raising the price.

The coordinated process repeats itself, but this time it is selling of the currency once it is at a particular price goal. The result is a sharp drop in the value of the cryptocurrency. As the group that pumps and dumps makes profit, other traders who invested in the crypto based on fake promises face huge loss.

Traders in these frauds use Telegram and Discord as their preferred method of communications. These groups cost between $50 and $250 per membership. In certain instances, traders are able to recommend the services to their friends and family members in order so that they can become members.

The Hong Kong-based Binance crypto exchange in Hong Kong is the most popular spot for these transactions because the exchange lists coins with small amounts with low liquidity. This allows them to be perfect targets to manipulate. Many traders have suffered losses of hundreds of dollars within a matter of seconds. They encourage weak traders to buy until they reach the price at which they want to be attained, and in many instances, the highest price is not achieved.

In the midst of the crypto market's period of bullishness, investors should remain conscious of the prevalence of crypto "pump and dump' scams. Find out what crypto coins will most likely become the target of thieves as well as what to look for in the signs of a scam using a pump and dump in the event that you come across one.

Although bitcoin is now an alternative asset with the help of regulated exchanges, a lot of institutions have invested in the cryptocurrency, along with its futures contracts, the majority of altcoins still struggle in a "wild west" sort of situation. The most reputable ones continue to be targeted as this was the situation during the time when attacks of 51% occurred against Ethereum Classic.

In the midst of crypto's efforts to make the next bull market Investors should know that many of the cryptocurrency with small trade volumes and market capitalization are at risk of being snatched by so-called pumps and dumps.

How To Identify A Pump And Dump Fraud

The fastest and easiest method to recognize the pump and dump plan is when a coin you don't know about dramatically increases without a justification. This can easily be seen by a price graph of the coin. As an example, Coincheckup set a benchmark of a 5% rise in just five minutes to be its benchmark.

In addition, if you come across sponsored news stories about an upcoming small cap cryptocurrency that is accompanied by an increase in online activity related to the particular cryptocurrency. This could be an indication that a pump is taking place.

If a coin that is barely recognized that is worth a market cap of a mere few million dollars, suddenly pops up all on Facebook and Twitter it is best to be on guard.

CFTC To Pay Pump And Dump Whistleblowers

In an effort to combat the unfortunate events that have been linked to the scheme to dump and pump the cryptocurrency market to stop the plight of crypto-related scams, the U.S.

Commodity Futures Trading Commission (CFTC) has stated that it will provide rewards for whistleblowers, who are the most involved in these dumped and pump organizations.

The CFTC earlier issued an earlier consumer advisory note. In the statement the Commission cautioned investors against cryptocurrency pump and dump scams to stop and cease. The same statement the CFTC informs investors that:

"customers should beware of pump-and-dump scams which can be found in traded or newly created 'alternative' digital currencies, virtual currency or tokens. Consumers should avoid buying digital currencies, virtual currency or tokens based upon the advice of social media or on sudden price increases."

To add to the caution in addition, the CFTC advised customers that they could be eligible for a financial amount of anywhere between 10% to 30% if those who belong to pump and dump groups provide authentic information, which could result in financial sanctions of $1million or higher.

It means that the CFTC will offer whistleblowers rewards if they share important information which leads to identifying and apprehending those who are who are behind these scams.

The idea of remunerating whistleblowers isn't a new idea. It's a practice that's already prevalent for traditional financial markets. However, it wasn't until in the year 2019 that United States regulators started eyeing the crypto market in this way.

Chapter 6: How To Avoid Pump And Dump Schemes

The pump and dump scheme is generally restricted to cryptocurrencies with a low level of volume of trading and market capitalization. So, it is possible to stay clear of cryptocurrencies that are not liquid to decrease the chance of being into the trap of pump and dump schemes. Also, not following the recommendations for investing on the internet or in paid-for stories will stop the possibility of suffering unavoidable losses because of such market manipulations.

A sudden increase in value without any verified evidence to support it is an indication that a new pump-and-dump strategy is in the making. Therefore, in the event that the chart shows that a pump has begun It is recommended to steer clear of such coins unless you've done extensive study of the cryptocurrency and the potential value it could have in the future.

Reddit as well as The BitcoinTalk forums are fantastic locations to research regarding these types of initiatives. In general, the cryptocurrency community is known to regulate itself and expose anyone who is committing fraud and thereby harm the reputation of the industry.

Directly contacting crypto companies in order to receive the answers you need is a fantastic method for conducting research on a particular coin prior to you decide to invest money into it. Additionally, research conducted by independent researchers can be utilized for making informed decisions about investments.

Malware Scams

Criminals target customers as well as businesses that have highly advanced technological devices. The most common method of spreading this technology is via emails and difficult-to-detect downloadings. This technology then secures the contents of the hard drive, which renders it impossible for users to gain access to their data.

The hackers attack unsuspecting customers who then claim the data they have stored is stored to be released for ransom. If the customer pays for it the ransom, it is not guaranteed that the information will be free of encryption. According to the Federal Trade Commission, after the malware has been installed on unaware computer users, hackers send a ransom message asking for payment.

Recent developments indicate that the criminals are more likely to use Bitcoin payments, or some other payment technique that's anonymous prior to they gain access to the victim's file. When the customer pays the ransom amount, there's little guarantee that the criminals will not demand more cash. The majority of times, criminals continue to ask for an additional amount from their victims.

Ransomware has been in use for a decade, however the severity and frequency of ransomware, such as CryptoLocker frauds are increasing. These scams have brought in millions of dollars for criminals. A research done by University of Kent revealed that 40percent of CryptoLocker victims have to pay the ransom.

The type of malware that is used in this case is very sneaky, and often hides itself as PDF files, JPEG pictures, Microsoft Office files, or any other harmless'safe file types. Numerous studies have been reported in the past suggesting that Facebook might be a significant source of the CryptoLocker malware. In the past, companies have suffered from the scams.

Not just individuals susceptible to these frauds. Servers and computers for entire companies are also lucrative target for the criminals. One example is a station for news located in Birmingham, Alabama, ABC 33-40, was infected with the Crypto Locker virus. Director of engineering at ABC 33-40, Ron Thomas, described his experiences of the infection.

Ron stated in an article in local media:

"You purchase this 300 Green Dot MoneyPak You are not able to use credit cards to buy the purchase, as it must be a cash purchase or a debit card. When they've claimed the funds then they can unlock your file. If these files were lost, it would have impacted more than 10 years worth of work done by various departments."

Crypto Ransomware Targeting Website Owners

Over the last few years, an increase in the number of cryptocurrency ransom frauds has been discovered. These scams target owners of websites, claiming they have their websites compromised and demand 1500-3000 dollars worth of bitcoins.

The perpetrators tell the story that the database on the site was snatched and, if the owner of the website fails to cooperate, they might expose the database or offer it to the top price.

Screenshot of the email.

In addition, they are threatening to employ the black-hat SEO techniques to degrade rankings of the website and make sure the credibility of the victim is damaged to the ire of Google as well as its customers. They do not provide any evidence to support the claims they make and do not respond to messages to make sure they aren't in any way negotiable.

"We have hacked your website and extracted your database."

The allegations are extremely worrying for those who have any kind of web-based site. However there are numerous instances of individuals receiving the same email, even though they don't own a site or domain.

Do your best to ask questions that can provide you with a real-time assessment whether the accusations are anything to worry about. Consider this: Is there any evidence of the claims of criminals? Do the emails contain authentic data that could indicate your site has been compromised, and the hackers have accessed the database? Does your website contain an existing database? What data is stored in your database?

Never Pay The Ransom

It is a bad idea to pay the ransom even though your system is completely encrypted due to ransomware isn't a good decision. For as it continues to be a practice for people paying ransoms, the frauds and ransomware continue to grow and become more deadly.

Unfortunately, when looking through the various bitcoin wallets that are linked to the attacks, it appears that there are many individuals who have been victimized by these scams and then paid ransom. One of the most notable wallets that were involved in various attacks received nearly $2000 in bitcoin payments. A different wallet was reported as being a victim of misuse more than 81 occasions.

Make sure you research the ransom email and Bitcoin ransom scams you come across. Similar scams have been utilized in the past to deceive users into believing that they were recorded on the computer. Sometimes, their passwords can be used to prove their identity that allows criminals to defraud the victims more.

Chapter 7: How To Avoid Malware Scams

There are a variety of strategies can be employed to prevent becoming a victim of scams involving malware. Begin by making sure that you back up all of your data often on various devices not linked to your PC. It is also possible to make use of cloud storage system that can be found on the internet.

Always look out for suspicious email or links that look suspicious. Beware of clicking on links and attachments sent by untrusted sending companies. You should consider using ads-filtering software which are usually free to use with internet browsers. These programs help you stay clear of clicking any shady hyperlinks that are generated by ads, whether by force or accidentally.

Authorities such as CFTC utilize information from scam victims to keep a close watch on the latest trends and alert people to any new strategies for crypto fraud. In particular, the number of reports about Bitcoin scams that involve blackmail fraud have grown over the last few times.

The emails usually claim that someone hacked your device, and then recorded your visit to various sites. They also threaten to release videos to family and friends families within a matter of hours in the event that you do not pay them to their bitcoin accounts. Pay nothing or delete the email as it's an obscene scam.

Some cybercriminals claim they have access to your camera or your computer, or are using clever software to get you killed. This is just a lie. But, sometimes, thieves be aware of one of your most recent or previous passwords and use it in their message to demonstrate they know it. When you come across this you need to change the password for that account. You should also change every password you use elsewhere.

Social Engineering Crypto Scams

A few attackers leverage their technological know-how and skills to gain access to secure computer systems. They aim to steal sensitive information. The malicious actors make every day, leading cybersecurity professionals to combat the activities of these criminals by creating innovative technologies to enhance security of networks.

However, different types of hackers employ other methods to get around security methods and security measures. They're known as social engineers' because they take advantage of the biggest weakness throughout all businesses: the human mind. They employ phone calls as well as other methods to entice users into giving access to confidential company details.

In its description, the term "social engineering" includes a broad range of nefarious actions. The primary types of attack are pretexting, phishing, as well as baiting.

Phishing

Phishing has been described as the most popular type of attack using social engineering which targets the crypto market today. On a broad level most frauds involving phishing attempt to achieve three objectives:

They employ short and misleading hyperlinks that lead visitors to malicious websites which contain the landing pages for phishing scams.

They collect personal data such as names, addresses, as well as Social Security Numbers.

These include threats, fear and a sense urgency, all of which attempt to con the people into reacting quickly.

Each phishing scam is unique to the other. There can be up to six kinds of phishing scams. Furthermore, some are not well-designed so that they suffer from spelling and grammar mistakes. All share the common goal of creating fake websites or forms in order to steal login credentials, as well as many other details about personal information.

A few phishing schemes employ compromised email addresses for sending out email attacks. The emails encourage recipients to read potential documents by clicking embedded URLs. The malicious URLs, encased by Symantec's Click Time URL Protection, will redirect users to compromised websites that provide various malicious URLs in different documents. Additionally, malicious URLs send users to fake websites that pretend to be authentic login sites. Then, they demand an amount of ransom, typically cryptocurrency, to release the login credentials back to the person who owns them.

Pretexting

Pretexting can be described as a form of social engineering, where criminals make up a false situation or an effective reason to steal the victims' personal details. These criminals typically claim they require certain details from the victims they are targeting for verification of their identities. However, they actually take the information and then employ it in subsequent attacks, or even engage in identity theft.

Highly advanced hacking techniques employ tactics that attempt to deceive the target into taking action that exploits a firm's physical and digital weaknesses. A criminal might impersonate outside IT auditors for services so they are able to convince the company's security personnel to let them gain access to the facility.

Although phishing attacks typically use the urgency and apprehension to gain advantage The main focus of pretexting attacks is in creating a false feeling of trust in the person being targeted. The attacker must make a plausible story that leaves be doubt about who they are targeting.

The practice of pretexting can take many types. However, the majority of attackers who engage in the tactic choose to disguise themselves as members of HR or finance employees. They can use disguises to attack executives at the top of the pyramid like the one which Verizon identified within the 2018 Data Breach Investigations Report (DBIR).

Baiting

Baiting can be compared to phishing attacks. But what separates these attacks apart from other forms of social engineering are their promise of products or services which the malicious actors make use of to entice their victims. Baiters use their promise of gratis giveaways, such as movie or music downloads for example, in order to lure uninitiated users into providing their login information.

The baiting attack is not restricted to only online scams. Criminals are also able to focus on engaging the curiosity of humans by using physical media. As an example, in July, KrebsOnSecurity reported on an attack which targeted local and state government departments across the US.

This operation delivered Chinese envelopes with postmarks, which consisted of a muddled letter with a compact disk (CD). Its goal was to increase people's curiosity, which led users to download the disc, and thus the malware on their computers. Following that, they demand for ransom payment in the Bitcoin.

Social Engineering Recommendations

Criminals who commit social engineering attacks utilize our human nature and drive to steal their target's details. In keeping this human-centric approach with an eye on the human, businesses are advised to support their staff in defending against these attacks.

In order to avoid scams using social engineering To avoid social engineering schemes, people should not open email from unknown sources make sure their laptops are secured and avoid giving offers from strangers with the benefit of doubt. In addition, they must buy antivirus software and be aware of the privacy policies of the business.

Chapter 8: Beware Of These Bitcoin Scams

In 2017, the explosive rise of Bitcoin has sparked interest from the masses in the most popular cryptocurrency. However, this increase in popularity came with negative consequences. A major issue the new investors faced when entering the market was an increase in quantity of cryptocurrency scams, false stories, and the retail investor who lost funds to scams.

In the wake of initial coin offerings (ICO) scandals to stolen and fraudulent use of wallets Regular users are able to become victims of criminals easily. The world appears to be an unregulated Wild West for investors without rules in the area. However, this doesn't have to be that way. Although there are a variety of opportunities in the market there are plenty of opportunities and very appealing to some.

It is, however, essential to stay vigilant and keep an eye for obvious signs of fraud. Stay clear of these traps to increase chances of success as well as safeguard your investment.

Hardware Wallet Theft

If you worry about security and privacy using a physical wallet that is a tangible device that holds private keys is a fantastic option. In general, they are designed to be as compact as keystrap USB drives These wallets have demonstrated to be a secure offline option for investors in crypto to secure their Bitcoin more.

There are however instances where gadgets have inherent weaknesses that render them vulnerable to hackers who could quickly steal the money of a user. It is among the many problems that impact the gadgets. Ofir Beigel said:

"One scam involves the sale of physical wallets to customers that have a pre-configured seed phrase concealed under scratch cards. The user who is new to the system is instructed that they must scratch off the credit scratch card ... then then set the wallet up with the seed that has been compromised. This opens a backdoor which lets hackers drain money when a wallet is active."

The scams that are causing havoc are becoming frequent. But they can be prevented by using wallets that are that are from reliable sources.

Exchange Scams

A majority of cryptocurrency are sold, bought through exchanges, despite the fact that they are not centralized. This allows users to search for the cryptocurrency they desire, the absence of a legitimate regulatory body oversees the actions of exchanges across the globe. Thus, the majority of investors are stuck and broke after the exchanges were signed up to are a trap.

A number of South Korean exchanges were exposed in the month of December 2017, which caused promises of tight guidelines by

South Korea's government. The scams that are exposed are easy to detect, but they could cost a lot of money when they're not snipped out of the way.

The most important red flag is the promise of unrealistic price promises. Anyone who promises massive discounts on bitcoin uses this tactic to entice unwitting users. Additionally, customers can look up websites' URLs for authenticity. Website addresses must always begin with HTTPS in order to prove that the data is secured. Surfing on unsecure sites isn't a good idea. But, savvy investors are able to avoid losses through being alert and looking for certain indications.

Shady and overnight exchanges are different types of scams involving cryptocurrency. What is their purpose? If, for instance, you are looking to swap your crypto token in exchange in exchange for a higher-performing digital asset, you'll seek ways to earn higher profit. The most effective way to accomplish this is to swap your cryptocurrency for one that performs better.

However, before you plunge into it, you should consider choosing an authentic and licensed cryptocurrency broker or exchange. It is possible to lose all the assets you have into an investment that seems too appealing to be real.

These exchanges are shady and follow the same pattern. If an investor is able to access crypto funds They find lower prices and make deposit coxed with shady brokers. They then ask what the business is doing The deal maker claims that he didn't upgrade the company and that the value fell, resulting in huge loss. The truth is this scenario, the deal-maker is stealing from the investors.

Fake ICOs

One of the greatest results of the cryptocurrency boom in 2017 was the rise in the first coin offer (ICO) to be a means for companies to raise funds. Since a variety of blockchain-based startups are coming on the scene with innovative concepts and projects customers can now support the businesses they love.

But, the massive growth in ICO opportunities has only led to an increase in scams. Fraudsters have devised numerous methods to steal bitcoins away from unwitting investors. The most popular strategy was the creating fake websites which appear to be ICOs. They also instruct clients to pay for bitcoins using an unreliable wallet. Sometimes it's the ICOs who are responsible.

As an example, Centra Tech, a blockchain-based project that is backed by a number of famous people, was sued in the United States. It was accused of presenting fake team members and deceiving investors and faking the products they offer. One way to steer clear of such schemes is to do extensive research, which includes dissecting the white paper as well as examining the people that is behind the business.

Chapter 9: Cloud Mining Scams

Mining is the only way to obtain new bitcoins without the need to buy or trade the bitcoins. But, in recent times, mining has turned into a resource-intensive process. Because of the distinctive ways in which bitcoins are extracted, it needs enormous quantities of processing power and electric power to make bitcoins. Therefore, it requires an enormous amount of money for mining bitcoins.

Nowadays, a lot of companies allow regular customers to lease servers to mine cryptocurrency for an agreed-upon amount. Certain companies offer "lifetime contracts' that keep identical costs, and also yield substantial profits. But, as the mining challenges increase and the investment yields lower amounts each time.

A few companies also make bold statements about their earnings but are not transparent about their actual costs and declining profits. Other companies have ponzi programs that can cause huge loss. It is crucial to research at opportunities and comprehend the potential risks and expenses associated with mining activity prior to making a decision to invest.

Multilevel Marketing

In the age of digital various multilevel marketing strategies have been introduced. The schemes provide investors with naive chances' to earn progressively more bitcoin. MLMs, which they're described, can be said to give quick profits from investments. But, they require higher profits in the hopes that they will earn more money.

OneCoin is among the companies with a notable reputation that was often exposed. Owners of the company were involved in a variety of suspicious operations. Investors were offered massive profits, luxurious goods and other perks in exchange for paying extra.

The company, however, provided limited information on its website, allowing users to read reviews from the Internet. It is important to read the fine print of a company and check whether their assertions are true and believable. Beware of scams as early as possible to safeguard your money investment.

In the present frenzied and buzz in crypto markets, it's best to stay vigilant and perform background checks prior to making a decision to invest. Markets are showing indications of maturity that could improve transparency and provide clearer guidelines. In spite of all one's initial step should always be conducting a thorough analysis to make sure that the investments will be profitable.

Blackmail

The use of blackmail has also grown in the amount of time that strangers harass customers to pay bitcoin to make the payment to pay for their outrageous extortions. One common tactic used in this type of scam is via email. Sender sends out a message saying that they've hacked into your server or computer and that they're operating via Remote Desktop Protocol (RDP).

The sender asserts that a key-logger had already been installed, and your camera on the internet was used to monitor you when you were performing something you would not want anyone else to know or see. The sender gives two choices for you to choose from sending bitcoin to hide the content or do nothing, and inappropriate content will be sent on your email address and then spread to all of your social media accounts.

Scammers employ stolen email lists as well as other information about users that was leaked to carry out their scam on millions of individuals.

Free Giveaways

Nowadays, information is all over the internet, and scammers search at ways to profit of their victims by offering cryptocurrency giveaways, especially bitcoin to pay small amount as registration costs or providing private information.

When you encounter the same on a site or social networking site, please declare the website or social network as a fraud to prevent others from becoming a to the same fate.

Impersonation

It's not difficult for scammers to make social media profiles and take on the personas of famous individuals. Additionally, some hackers take over celebrities' accounts to trick followers into giving Bitcoin, as occurred recently on Twitter. They don't speak until the person they want to impersonate posts content.

The person who is impersonating it responds by sending follow-up messages, and calling to take action, such as a no-cost giveaway. They use an account that is almost like the original poster or writer. The appearance of the author is speaking to this.

However fakes may try using the same fake accounts to fool others via direct and private messages to take some kind of step in an effort to steal or cheat. Beware of free giveaways, and if you receive odd requests from people in your circle make sure you confirm that the request is genuine through a variety of methods of communications.

Phishing Websites And Emails

Watch out for emails that appear to be coming from a company are used by you and asking you to take different actions, such as changing passwords, or clicking through to provide some kind of communication regarding your account.

It is often difficult to discern the distinction between an email from a scammer who will try to get users to take down their accounts as well as a genuine one, being sent by an item or service you utilize.

If you're unsure you should double-check whether the message is authentic through ensuring you send your message to the business via the email address for contact that is on their website. It is possible to call them over the phone or contact them via their the official social media profiles.

Phishing sites are frequently associated with emails that are phishing. These emails may link to a fake website that can be designed to obtain login credentials, or perhaps induce users to download malware. Do not install software or log to websites unless you're absolutely certain it's authentic and not fake.

The websites that are phishing also show up as ads for search engines, as well as on marketplaces in-app that are used by various mobile phones. Make sure you're not downloading an app that is fake as well as clicking on a paid hyperlink to a fake website.

Ponzi And Pyramid Schemes

Do not participate in offers which involve a group of people who give you a guarantee of reward as a condition of an initial money deposit. It's known as a Ponzi scheme in which deposits made by future investors will be used exclusively for the payment of prior investors. The result is that the majority of investors lose lots of cash.

Pyramid schemes guarantee the participants a return based on the amount of people they allow to sign up. This allows the scheme to increase in size, but does not result in any significant reward for those who join or those they invite to be joined the scheme.

Do not invite your friends and family to earn rewards or profits from the purchase of a product or service and refrain from contributing capital to other people to accelerate the procedure.

Prize Giveaways

Similar to the giveaways that are free The scams associated with prize giveaways fool people into taking engaging in a certain way or giving a great deal of personal information. Examples include providing the address, number along with email and names to win prizes. This technique allows hackers to attempt using available data to open accounts pretending to be the account owner.

Pump And Dump

Do not trust any person who promises individuals to invest with the claim that they are aware of what bitcoin's value is going to be in the near future. The"pump and dump" scheme people try to increase prices to get rid of their assets to make an income.

Automated Trading Systems

Because of the volatile nature of cryptocurrency, marketers look for every opportunity to profit. Most often, the main focus is to speculate on the cost difference in different exchanges.

They are thought of as a scam because exchanges typically have lengthy process of withdrawal. Additionally, they cost quite a bit to trade bitcoins or ether with the fiat currency. It is generally accepted that cryptocurrency arbitrage imposes a significant cost on the user without guaranteeing any gains. Most likely, it will result in the loss of money. They also require an extended time to complete so anything could occur during the time.

Ransomware

This kind of malware may blocks access to devices in the event that a user is unable to pay an amount of ransom using bitcoin or any other cryptocurrency that is chosen. If you encounter such an incident seek out trusted experts in computer security to help remove the malware instead of paying a ransom.

Experts suggest that you be aware of the software that you download to your devices, specifically those that require administration access. Be sure to confirm that the software you're downloading is authentic that is not fake and impersonating an authentic one that has been employed program previously.

Chapter 10: Scam Coins

Make sure you are cautious about making investments in alternative currencies (altcoins) as there are fake coins. They make investors put their money into discount coupons or sales. Many times, fake coins are sold on an attractive website, and claim that they have a large community, creating the fear of losing out effects on those who come across the scam.

This strategy allows the initial holders to boost prices and dump after they have resigned their positions in order to earn the possibility of making a profit. A few coin that don't have huge communities might have airdrops that give away complimentary coins to the people who sign up to their community.

This strategy allows scam coins to show their projects by presenting a inflated number of traction statistics which make investors believe that they're missing something as they begin thinking about purchasing the coins. Certain scam coins might use the term "bitcoin" to fool or deceive users into thinking that there's a real connection.

If in doubt, reach For Help

The initial step before using any cryptocurrency-related website or platform is reaching an experienced individual. You could do this by posting to the Reddit cryptocurrency forum or asking a tech-savvy acquaintance about the website. If you ever have further questions, speak to the reputable crypto experts, who can warn you if you're about investing in a cryptocurrency fraud.

A majority of scam websites display an attractive and professional looking website that comes filled with images, logos as well as login and testimonials. It is possible that they will come up with an entirely new logo or attempt to copy a trusted name. Utilize a tool known as WhoIs Lookup to find out who owns the domain. of the domain. Most often, crooks create domains on their own.

The countries which have become a notorious hotbed of scammers are Nigeria, North Korea, and India. However, scams involving crypto have been popping up across all over the world because of the decentralized nature of digital currencies. Physical locations of the currency do no longer matter.

Examining the cryptocurrency scamming platforms yields no results as these criminals attempt to conceal their identities. As servers can be located in any part of the world and they can appear that they're located operating from Los Angeles, California while they're operating out of Sydney, Australia. Therefore, any investigation could end at a dead end.

The most efficient method to judge whether a website is genuine is to use images.google.com, a reverse image search. Images that claim to represent "the team in action" or office buildings that are official in nature typically come from different websites and sources.

Watch out for the fake testimonials, which hackers edit to look authentic. If you take a closer look at them, you'll find that these are fakes with fake identities, or using celebrity identities and pictures. If you notice all of the characteristics listed above, then it is an online scam.

Unfortunately, not everyone is exposed to the 'investment options' security in place. Through the live chat window that is available 24 hours a day across all these websites the customer service representatives are said to provide interest for deposits. The quicker one can make a deposit, the more amount of interest they will earn.

When a deposit is made, the balance on the internet is adjusted to reflect the "profits" but eventually, it is impossible to cash out what clients are entitled to. Unaware victims forfeit their "investment".

They target novices through a linkage with celebrities or companies with a good reputation for example Bill Gates, Jeff Bezos,

Tesla, Elon Musk among others. A Redditor named Pythagorean0503 has highlighted the following:

"Youtube has been flooded by this lately. It's a shocker to think that YouTube is able to immediately censor negative comments on different SJW (social justice warrior) subjects, but they have no idea of the bitcoin scams are spreading by the algorithms. I have seen one in the name of Linus Torvalds, and another for Elon Musk in the last few days, but didn't try to transfer any cash."

Image Is Everything

Criminals are targeting people who believe that cryptocurrency is an easy-to-make-money scheme. With the numerous stories published about 'bitcoin millionaires," it's not difficult to understand why websites that have a shaky sense of authenticity still attract ignorant investors.

Be aware that there is no evidence-based quick-money schemes that promise to make you rich in the cryptocurrency area or in any other sector of the world's financial system. These are fraudulent schemes. It is possible to generate some excitement about investing, as the fraudulent scammers claim isn't possible without running the Ponzi scheme. The majority of criminals don't have to think over coming up with complicated plans due to the flexibility of bitcoin.

Instead, they lead users through the buying bitcoin and sending procedure using reputable solutions such as Huobi and Coinbase but then stop when the trade has been concluded with success. Even though a site might appear authentic, that doesn't necessarily mean it is legitimate. A lot of crypto frauds are legitimate and even individuals or simply connect themselves to discussions on social media sites that offer Bitcoin for free.

Cybercriminals target people who are on non-financial social media platforms such as Twitter or Instagram. In particular, they steer clear of legitimate financial websites and message boards. In the end, they profit from our naivety and greed.

What Can You Do?

If you've already transferred money to an incorrect bitcoin account, it's likely that it has already been refunded. Crypto scams can easily withdraw money by buying local crypto and then selling it in transaction that takes place in person. If you find out that you've made a mistake and inform your bank like Coinbase and Coinbase, they could try to stop your transactions, however, it's not often successful.

Beware of sites offering quick profits or high interest rates for your investments. Any person who claims that they will be rich in a short time can only talk about themselves, if they are able to defraud you and other investors who were not expecting it.

Chapter 11: The most common scams and hacks

They aren't your keys. Not your cash.

Make sure you are safe.

The original intention was to jump directly into the heart of the information on assessing the legitimacy of any new ventures. In the beginning, I planned to go through common scams and hacks due to the fact that these all appeared very obvious in their attempt to get.

I was mistakenly thinking that only a few individuals would ever fall for such fraudulent phishing scams. It's true that we've avoided them for a long time on Web2 and the majority of methods are similar to those used with Web3 do you think?

It's a pity that I'm very sorry to say that I'm wrong.

The months prior to this post In the months leading up to this guide, there were numerous scams which are able to fool even the most knowledgeable crypto-traders and NFT collectors. As an example...

Cybercriminals are targeting exchanges as well as platforms in order to steal valuable funds

Hackers discovered a flaw inside Li Finance allowing them to extract around $600,000 worth cryptocurrency taken from 29 different wallets.

In a non-technical manner Hackers discovered an exploit which allowed the hacker to swap before bridges.

Then, following the theft hacker immediately changed the currency stolen into ETH and then transferred the funds into their personal accounts.

Making use of Discord to trick holders

In the next section, we'll explore communities to aid in the evaluation of the latest projects. One of the most important methods to employ to accomplish the purpose is Discord.

Discord is often the preferred commenting and messaging channel used for several Web3 projects.

The scammers are aware of this.

Fraudsters are targeting the official Discords and are sharing harmful links. Through this, hyperlinks appear to be coming from the founders of the Discord project. So, holders of the project can trust the hyperlink.

The scammers can either crack the passwords of Discord administrators or utilize applications and tools with access to the chat as a way to share hyperlinks within chat.

The method is used to get access to very valuable assets, such as BAYC. Particularly from Chinese actor and musician Jay Chou.

In the end the result is that this strategy has led the way to billions of dollars worth of loss of assets.

What can you do to make sure you stay away from fraudulent scams?

I could go on about these types of scams, hacks, and phishing scams. The Decent Reviewsblog and the newsletter with stories about these issues each day (and you'll receive all the most recent information delivered to your inbox when you join us on DecentReviews.co).

Instead of continuing to describe what transpired, we'll shift our attention to ways you can do to fix this.

It is essential be sure you're protected and vigilant throughout the day. Most of these attacks are targeted at your tools and platforms that which you use. There is no way to ensure the security of these tools and platforms.

The only thing you need to do is be very careful and extremely critical of everything you read on Web3. Wild West of Web3.

Below are some steps I'd suggest to safeguard your possessions.

Make sure you have a cold bank account

In general, there are two different types of wallets available to keep all of your Web3 assets.

Hot wallets such as MetaMask are only available digitally and can be found on websites such as a browser extension.

They are also known as cold wallets (or Hardware wallets) typically will require verification of transactions that require a physical division that you hold. They're both physical and digital.

The bottom line is that hot wallets are more vulnerable to attacks and hackers due to the fact that they're digital. When someone has the access of your account they'll be able to empty it in minutes.

The hard wallets come with a built-in element of a physical key. You'll need login codes for your wallet and to keep the physical key to verify any transactions or trades.

Below is an easy visual to explain.

The majority of hard wallets have two-factor authentication. This is what makes them safer. More specifically this makes it more difficult for scammers to take your funds with your permission.

If you're storing valuable assets or something that you're keeping until the value appreciates you should try storing it in a safe wallet for added protection. Also, make sure the wallet is exclusively used to store your items.

However, what is Crypto Exchange Insurance?

Some might argue that moving your money to the cold bank account which has to be approved by a manual process to all transactions is not worth the burden. It's a fair point.

In the end, all of the top cryptocurrency exchanges offer some kind of protection in the event in the event of fraud or hacking. Why not put your coins in an exchange which is protected against losses.

This is a feasible option when it's a real currency as well as a reputable exchange such as Binance. If you're holding one-of-a-kind BAYC, once you're gone the moment it's gone, it's gone.

This isn't like Bitcoin that a platform might potentially replace by adding more Bitcoin.

If you've had to claim insurance on anything and you've heard about the fact that insurance companies will always be looking for reasons to not pay. If you glance at the exchanges which have been compromised typically, they pay some - but not all victims.

Li Finance example above Li Finance example above made 27 of the 29 victims whole following the incident when we wrote this article.

Make sure that everything is checked

Imagine that you're on a project's Discord when you spot an authentic mod post the link of a fresh website that you've never heard of previously.

It's said to verify an asset's authenticity, to be entered in a contest for the release of a new item and even to join to your Discord account. The only thing you need to do is click the URL and then sync your wallet.

Each of them could all be genuine. But, don't take any of them for granted and make sure to verify every assertion that they're making.

Are the sites that they're linking to being belonged to the company that owns it?

Do you think BAYC provide a link to an not affiliated site, in order to ask you to transfer funds from your account? Unlikely.

If it's not one of the sites that they control, is it a project that they've approved to collaborate with? working with? Like, for instance, BAYC is linking to Deadfellaz? If yes, then is the link-to legitimate?

If not Is the website an established player in the area? Like POAP.xyz?

Are there discussions of this happening in multiple locations?

Marketing for projects must be effective. If this is a legitimate partnership it will the possibility of announcing it on the project's website or social profiles, among other things. Chances that hackers are able to gain access to several channels are very slim.

Does it feel good?

If you don't like something take your instincts into consideration. Contact confirmed project participants to find their thoughts and opinions as well as insight into the shady messages.•

The good news is that many organizations are cognizant of this and getting ready to establish easy checklists for users to check any messages. Like this message is from XanaMetaverse is available on Twitter.

Chapter 12: Team and founders

Which companies are you putting your money into?

Make sure you know who you're sharing a the bed with.

Imagine that you are the VC company and you are thinking of buying a new brand. Do you plan to go with the hype and sign an enormous check since the twitter-sphere is blowing over the company?

Perhaps. However, it is not likely.

The majority of VCs will have an extensive checklist of what they'll be looking to prove the value of their decision to invest. One of them is the founders. The team will look at issues like...

The morality of their character

* Their background and experiences

* Their motivation, their goal, and vision

* Specialists in important sectors of growth and operation

If you are considering investing into a brand new Crypto or NFT initiative, you have be looking for the same traits. In the end, you are making a commitment to the company as well as the venture.

However, simply saying the same thing doesn't help anybody. Let's translate the above topics into context and discuss how to examine them.

Before getting into these areas One thing I look out for whenever new initiatives are launched. It's...

Does the project have a negative impact on the team that started it?

If the team's founders hide with pseudonyms, anonymous addresses or even fake names this is a red flag. Because of the nature of cryptocurrency payments as well as the shady owners of their wallets, they are possible to be able to steal funds belonging to other individuals.

If you don't know about the originators this makes it easy for them to steal your money.

The majority of successful ventures include public and visible the founders and team members. It's hard to come up with only two instances where this isn't the case (BAYC as well as Bitcoin).

In addition to BAYC as well as Bitcoin being a secret or unidentified founders is a red flag and an issue to be aware of.

Being aware of who is behind the project makes the subsequent steps of checking feasible.

Moral Character

It's a difficult one to assess. If you are familiar with one of the founders, it is worth taking the time to study the background of their team members.

It is important to search for items such as...

Notes from the media (good/bad press)

* Interviews (podcasts video, podcasts or even written)

* Review (from employees, customers etc.)

If you discover a record of questionable moral conduct and numerous reviews of their negatives which aren't addressed, and appear authentic, or tales of the shady actions they've committed Ask if you're satisfied to pay them.

Most likely, you won't.

Experiential and historical background

This can be a lot easier to study.

If you are familiar with the group, it is possible to look up the previous work history of their team. You're trying to find any relevant work experience within the industry.

In fact, currently there are a variety of NFT games that are being designed by the new studios.

The fact that this is the case doesn't pose a problem. It is possible to start a modern marketing company today and yet achieve great results since I've got more than 10 years of experience.

But, if you spend the time to research the past of some of the game studio's founders and directors, you'll see that they've had no knowledge of building games.

Many come from an artistic background. They have shifted into the game industry through the process through NFT sales.

The artwork plays a major role for a successful game play. However, there's beyond art-related style that can ensure a successful game.

In addition, if the founding team has little experience with game theory, or in creating engaging stories, mechanics etc. it's a cause for concern.

In simple terms, it's an extremely signal of caution. The process of creating a winning game is a challenge. Experienced game development studios have a tendency to fail.

Everyone loves to be in the fight for the weak and encourage individuals who have aspired to succeed. However, the tale of the initial founder who made billions of dollars with a subject they've had never had any experience with is limited to just a few people in the past.

Do you believe in someone who has none of the core competencies in your financial transactions?

I don't.

Their motivation, their vision, determination

What is the goal they are hoping to accomplish with this particular project?

The most successful Web3 projects are those with a clear and ambitious goals.

The people who created it aren't doing it solely for cash and to assist in solving actual problems, or create innovative things for the people who hold it.

When a plan offers a plan that is likely to create real good in all of humanity, the probability that it will succeed in the long run is increased.

It is important to consider what value tangible the venture can bring. It is best if it provides a genuine ROI for investors.

If there's not any benefit other than the simple fact that it's being used for glory, the odds of success are slim.

Expertise in key domains

It is based on the knowledge gained of core roles mentioned previously. Some projects are successful even though the creators themselves do not have any prior experience relevant to the job.

You're seeking clever founders that can create a team of specialists.

Let's say, for example, the release of an NFT game that is released on Ethereum. Ethereum blockchain.

On their team there are no experts in game or ETH blockchain experts. What are their chances of their success?

The smallest of the three.

Take a look at a different idea that was created by a veteran business owner. The owner recognizes their own weaknesses and tries to bridge the gap.

In the event that they do not have prior experience, they head out to hire an experienced blockchain specialist, who was also a the former Ubisoft game developer.

What are the odds that you can bet on to be successful?

There's no need to think about it, right?

It's the same for every initiative. Look beyond the founder and determine the team they've assembled with the right people in order that can help them achieve the goals they set for themselves. Each of the key areas of growth and operation should be staffed by a knowledgeable team member.

The founding team is vitally crucial

You want to ensure that you be confident in the group that is creating this plan. As well as in regards to their ethics and abilities.

The rules above aren't only a problem, but. A solid morally upright leader with an eye for the future is able to hire technical experts.

Although a team of experts with a track record of scams, those who operated previously aren't to be trusted.

The key is to find the connections and then making a decision based on all the data.

In the next section in the next chapter, we'll look specifically at the artwork of NFTs as well as their design.

Chapter 13: NFT artwork

Indices of success that are subjective

What are the signs of a good art work?

The topic of this chapter on NFT artwork. This is a fascinating topic. The general rule is to categorize NFT art work into two groups. Generative and non-generative.

Let's examine the latter in the first.

The art of generating in NFTs.

A lot of people are only aware about the work that generates of massive NFT collections. A few people are enthralled by the generative style that you can find in collections such as BAYC as well as CryptoPunks. There are a lot of people who aren't convinced.

It's not an issue. The art world is a subjective. The things that one person is passionate about, one person hates.

You can take CryptoPunks as one of the most lucrative NFT inventions. The concept is simple, pixels. Many love it, however some people complain that they aren't able to comprehend or appreciate the work.

Most of the time users use their art generative as profiles in a variety of places on the internet. The thing that a majority of people actually like is when the work features a unique design or feature.

It is evident that many of these pieces of generative art can be constructed by the fusion of a variety of designs that are templated. Certain design elements are more commonly used in comparison to other design elements. Many people would rather be able to get the most rare components to gain publicity purposes.

On platforms like OpenSea On marketplaces such as OpenSea, you are able to discover how scarce the various elements from each NFT are.

The collection as a whole as well as its utility can attract a large number of people into an undertaking however, most times you'll discover individuals looking for more rare features.

The basic principle is demand and supply. The more scarce an item is, the more people are willing to spend for it. Also, it's common for groups of people who share unique characteristics. Further details on this will be forthcoming.

However, the main point is the art here is more about the bragging rights of its creator and rarity, rather than art.

Non-generative art

On the other hand There are also NFTs that focus on artwork. Consider, for instance the work " 5000 days of Beeple".

Beeple is a well-known digital artist. His image above is a collage made up of more than 5000 hours of his work.

The chance that a person would purchase something specifically to be used for art is higher than that of an generative piece of art.

The issue you'll face in this case is that art is highly subjective and therefore hard to judge as a long-term worth. The Beeple work is simpler since the artist enjoys a large audience and a standing.

What is the best way to evaluate the quality of artwork?

Purchase of non-generative or generative art works is fine. You should, however, look at the long-term view of the art.

All of it is an opinion (making this an extremely difficult subject to analyze) It is important to consider questions such as...

* Do I love this painting?

* Are there others who appear enjoy this art work?

* What is it about this article that's "collectable"

Chapter 14: Community

Who will be your classmates?

Make wise choices, or there's no benefit.

A majority NFT collections as well as Cryptocurrencies are part of a community.

There are some that have been designed, and others develop naturally when there's an assemblage of individuals with the same goal and interest. No matter the cause, the community element is crucial to know what you're bringing to the table.

This is where the real value of a lot of projects is and is easy to understand. A strong community will to propel the NFT project or cryptocurrency into the status of a blue chip. If the wrong community is in place, it will cause a swift conclusion to the collection's

Where can I locate communities with similar interests?

It is generally recommended to consider one of two locations to evaluate the project's community.

The most popular option is Twitter since it offers the public with a clear view of the community that is part of it and its owners.

To locate the communities of the project in question the only thing you need to do is type in the word. It will provide you with an update of the most recent and most relevant information to the.

It is recommended to sort this data by the most recent rather than top, to see all the information, not only the ones that are most active with the comments.

Alongside the public messages on social media You should also be aware of private community. Most Web3 communities are able to use Discord to communicate with their community.

On an organization's website, they'll usually have a no-cost community open to anyone who is interested in joining. Find the following image.

Click here to sign up to their private, free community. Many of the functions that are reserved to holders are locked out however, you do not need this to comprehend the general experience yet.

Analyzing the community

If you've come across individuals using Twitter or even the Discord community, you should join them. Be sure to review the messages from previous years and join on a couple of conversations.

While researching various projects, Here's what I've seen that makes more secure, better investments...

* They're friendly and supportive.

* They are focused on the personal goals and community.

They discuss future goals, and they discuss how they'll utilize their memberships to achieve them.

Compare that with simple rug pulls as well as scams you'll come across...

* Focus solely on pricing and value of the floor.

Too many instances in reference to "to the moon!"

Focusing on the ways they might increase the cost of their products and discussing when they should decide to sell

Today, even the top communities might focus on the second. Everyone likes earning profits. The knowledge that you're a involved in a popular and well-known project is sure to lead many to be proud.

It's fine. So so long as this isn't the main goal of the people in the community. If this is the case, it's a sign that most people are only looking to sell and make money.

If the vast majority of people sell to make quick money What happens to the worth of the venture? It will become a transactional asset instead of being an investment. This means it will not hold any worth over the long-term.

The focus on price at the floor and not considering the best time to sell is a short-term approach. This leads to gains only for a few known individuals (usually the people who founded it) however, it robs others of any worth.

One of the best examples of a properly-designed and well-managed NFT project that I'm currently a member of called Leveling Up Heroes. It's not an attempt to promote them however it's just an example of what you can do to make it successful.

Below is an image of two reactions that people are posting in the open.

You can see how all of them are positive as well as supportive of the idea as well as other people who have embraced the idea.

It's interesting to see the emphasis on goals for the future.

You can see how the people are having fun and embracing the openness.

Notice, too, the fact that none of these positive messages originate from well-known influencers, or even shill accounts. They are just ordinary people who express their gratitude with sincerity.

Finding the people you want to be with

If you discover a program with a focus on community benefit over time You must determine whether they're the ones you want to work with.

That's that they're unified by the same set of beliefs that they share. I signed up to Leveling Up Heroes because it's an organization with a large number of people who want to improve their business.

If there were the perfect, supportive NFT project specifically for single moms could it be suitable for me as a male who doesn't have children?

No.

While I may consider it a good idea, I won't benefit from purchasing the project. It is important to ensure that the groups that you participate in have a group that is similar to the people whom you want to emulate.

The idea may seem incredibly stupid and evident, yet it's very easy to get swept up with the excitement of an idea because you love things that resemble the design or the intended use.

If the purpose and the community's vision is completely different from your values, circumstances or objectives There's likely to be very little worth gaining from it. If everyone joins organizations and groups that aren't able to contribute to, the initiative will end up becoming not worth the effort.

If you've come across a project that you're intrigued by however, it doesn't always have any direct benefit for you however, you may be able to contribute to it through other avenues. I'd suggest keeping purchase spots open for people who directly gain by joining.

There's nothing stopping you from supporting them to increase their visibility and reach by acting as a public advocate or sharing their latest updates.

Chapter 15: Utility

Be sure to get the most value for your money

Does this really work?

The community aspect is certainly a major aspect of every Web3 initiative, one more important aspect to be looking for is functionality. Particularly, what could I make use of this investment to be useful in my daily life.

If it's not used in any way What are the odds it'll hold its value and make a good investment?

Low.

It is essential to ensure the product you're purchasing will have real-world use. It could be any utility. Some of the more typical ones to search for include...

* Admission to online classes (NFTs)

* Collateral to Fiat loans (NFTs or Cryptocurrency)

* Gain access to actual workplace occasions (NFTs)

* Membership in a group of peer (NFTs or Cryptocurrency)

• Ability to exchange for similar physical items (NFTs)

The ability to stake real, compounding returns (Cryptocurrency)

The appreciation of value will create a traditional money-making investment (NFT or Cryptocurrency)

The projects that have the potential to be more than just innovative ideas will keep their worth for a longer time.

It's also a lot more difficult to falsify if you're providing the possibility of accessing goods or services IRL. It's also much easier to detect frauds. The real functionality is based on readily verified credentials as well as organizational demands.

As an example, suppose you are working on a plan...

* Hosts an event, and you are able to verify the availability of venues and speaker confirmations

The community is available You can test it out via the public channels

* It can be used to secure loans as collateral, it is just a matter of checking with the lending company to see to see if they are willing to would accept the asset.

The real-world application generally allows for greater checks. In the event of a legitimate application, it will assist in preserving the value of the asset.

The key is ROI.

What it comes down to is the issue...

"What's the ROI of buying into this project?".

The real-world utility simply is an opportunity to make sure that the owners get more out of the investment than they paid for it at beginning.

The long-term benefit means that other individuals would like to move in and become part of the community. The value of your asset grows as does the demand for it.

If there isn't any profit from the initial investment then no one will to be interested in joining this project again in the near future. Thus, the worth of the asset you own will most likely remain the same and will, more likely decrease.

It's likely that you'll have your wallet stuffed with PFPs as well as coins from abandoned initiatives that you're not able to hire someone to remove from your hands.

Let's take a look at some instances of projects that have excellent return on investment.

Here are a few of them.

Below are a few instances of practical utility using well-known Web3 projects. In the beginning, we'll look at a couple of NFT projects.

NFT projects with high utilitarian

The Leveling Up Heroes includes a physical book, and access to the community, as well as IRL networking occasions

Crypto packaged Goods provides the opportunity to invest in member companies and have access to business coaches

VeeFriends provides users the opportunity to attend an upcoming Gary Vee meeting

All of the above are NFT collections that possess the potential to be of use in real life, meaning they can be able to hold value for a longer duration. If this utility is sustained and maintained, their value will only grow.

Good utility for cryptocurrencies

Ethereum - Excellent support for DeFi and the network is utilized to host a variety of decentralised apps

SOL A promising cryptocurrency and network that has better capacity and speed than Ethereum

ADA It is part of the Cardano network. It has smart contract software similar to Ethereum however, it uses the proof of stake to verify transactions which makes it faster and consumes less energy

Whichever project you're making an investment in, ensure that it has some sort of practical use.

If you're able to use utility, you're more likely to see an ROI that is positive and this means your project will be less likely to fail.

Chapter 16: Influencers

With whom are they working?

You can judge a person's character by the name they run.

Influencer marketing has been proven to be a reliable technique for increasing impact. I've written about it multiple times in my Growth models, and I've utilized it with great success for a variety of brands that I've spoken to.

The impact of successful influencer-driven campaigns isn't going under the radar in the world of business too. Numerous Web3 projects rely on influential people to help spread the word.

The issue isn't that brands look to influencers to spread the word but rather that a lot of consumers are prone to blindly following the guidance of an influential persona. Even when the advice they receive is clearly bad.

It allows the proliferation of scams and rug-pulling projects that make money off unsuspecting, well-mannered folks.

If you're looking for a idea to invest in go through the different influencer-related promotions and collaborations they've run. The focus isn't on information about the contents of the promotions as such, but instead considering the people they're working with.

We're trying to form an evaluation of the business they maintain. If you come across influencers or celebrities that have promoted the idea of your new venture look at the influencers with these guidelines.

Do they have a solid understanding of Crypto?

Many people who have any kind of crowd are embracing Web3 promotions because of the amount of money that can be earned.

The majority of influencers who promote particular projects do not have prior knowledge or understanding in the field of Crypto and blockchain. They wouldn't be able to tell whether they're promoting fraud or otherwise. What they are really concerned about is receiving this sweet, sweet promotional benefit.

Influencers who are associated with something totally unrelated to Crypto is for me untrue. Look at the many scam stories connected with Jake Paul as an illustration.

Jake Paul is not known for his understanding of Blockchain or crypto tech. Jake Paul is known as an influential person. Therefore, the odds that the recommendations he makes will succeed over the long run are very low. However, the odds of paying a large sum of money for promoting something are extremely significant.

It's all about how and when they're marketing products. If they were promoting the use of a tooth-whitening product and today there's a fresh NFT collection, then you shouldn't trust them.

Do you believe them?

Similar to studying the original team. Consider if the person you're researching is someone you'd be able to trust.

If they have a questionable moral history then you may want to consider staying clear of the projects they endorse.

I hate to judge the man, but you think of Jake Paul. I would not trust him to keep my Ice cream. There are always scams or rug-pulls as well as some shady ploys. Whatever he's engaged in I consider highly suspect.

What kind of campaigns have they pushed in the recent past?

We can tell the grain from the shreds. It's evident that many of fraudulent projects hit with the same inf uencers to get promotional campaigns.

If someone continues to promote carpet pulls or frauds, be sure to steer off.

Use this tweet by @zachxbt to serve as an illustration. He criticizes @AltcoinGordon's constantly promoting projects which have that have been proven fraudulent.

This can be surprisingly simple to study. All you need to do is look up the profile of their company and share history to find specific keywords.

Visit the social networks search engine, then focus on the account and sort by terms such as...

"To the Moon"

* $

* Whitelist

* Sold out

* Investment

* Miss out

or if they are inclined to utilize a particular words in their advertisements look up that language for examples of past promotions using a similar languages.

Here's a short and simple information on how to research their previous promos.

Investigating the past promotional efforts of an influencer

First, find the last time they were promoted.

Check out the influencer's publications, social media accounts or web-based past to find out what was that they recently featured.

It's not difficult to come across.

It's important to find something that will get people enthusiastic about your idea and entice people to invest in it.

For ease of use to find the terms mentioned earlier or any other which could be used to convince people that it's a wise investment.

2. Check the amount of money that is in that asset

You can then go to a site similar to Trading View (there's a full list of possible tools towards the end chapter) which will enable you to assess the worth of the investment as time passes.

You're searching for something similar to the following.

If you influencer has been promoting this or...

Then, just as it begins to rise in value

In the course of rising

... Then does not mention it at all on or following the fall The smart money is on it being just a pumps and dump.

They may have used the followers of their group to increase values before selling off at the top to earn a substantial profits.

3. Final check

If you're not certain check social media to find any references to the person or the item they're advertising.

It's incredible how transparent and truthful people who've fallen victim to frauds have been. I would also suggest following individuals such as @Zachxbt as their insight could prove invaluable.

If you cannot find any evidence of pump or dumps and nobody has ever mentioned any scams in the past, you're completely safe.

But, there is no way to be 100% secure and you must be wary of those on the web.

Chapter 17: Tokenomics

Who is the owner of what?

Are they trying to cover up an e-scam?

It is possible to get a first notion of the longer-term goals of a project looking through the tokenomics.

If you're unfamiliar that tokenomics is the under the scenes mechanism of how the project works.

* If the tokenomics have been properly designed, this project will succeed.

* If the designs aren't well thought out the chances are that they'll fail.

If they're constructed to only favors the creators, then you ought to stay from them.

There are certain items you need to search for in tokenomics, which we'll discuss in the near future.

To begin, I'd like to discuss how you can discover the breakdowns of tokenomics.

Locating tokenomics breakdowns

Most projects have some kind of whitepaper which outlines specifics of the project.

There is usually an easy hyperlink to the whitepaper on the site of the project. There are additional tools, such as Whitepaper.iowh ch collate whitepapers to make it easier for you to analyze.

If your project isn't listed on an outline of the project, visit the website for a type of route map, as they usually has the information you're after.

Use the example below of DeadFellaz. There isn't a whitepaper available, but they do publish updates on their blog on Medium.

If you can find the details of their activities then what exactly are you searching for?

Supply

Supply is the most important aspect you must consider in the development of any Web3 project, or investment or business.

What you're actually trying to determine is if the project has enough production to allow the venture to be able to sustain its the value.

If creators overflow the market, the price will fall.

Compare the differentiating factors of Bitcoin and Doge to illustrate.

Bitcoin was invented with a strict cap. The Bitcoin network will be limited to the limit of 21 million Bitcoin. The release is in a manner that decreases in half every 4 years approximately.

It creates a release calendar which looks like the below. After 21,000,000 Bitcoin circulated, no additional Bitcoin will be issued.

It's also estimated that there are around 19 million in the world. This means we're close to reaching the higher limit.

Doge however isn't capped at any point. It was first launched with 100 billion coins. It is currently approximately 5 billion every year..

Every year, the Doge is afflicted by approximately 5% inflationary pressure. In the long run, this could reduce the worth of the Doge.

There is the steady decrease in value when you take a look at the last year's Doge's worth.

If there's only a small amount of stock and demand, expect an inflationary strain that reduces value to be lesser severe.

If the intent by the designers is to keep minting new NFTs, coins, or any other asset that has the same value or are similar to their predecessors then you should expect an increase in inflation that will slowly diminish the worth.

Demand

An insufficient supply isn't the only thing to be thought about.

The idea of minting only 100,000 pictures of my left foot for NFTs, or having a inventory of

100,000 coins with no function will not guarantee the highest value.

Demand is an important aspect of value overall.

Similar to what we said earlier that there must be some sort of utility. It can take many types, but anything that is not utility-based will not last or appreciate in value.

Although it isn't an all-inclusive listing, there are a few possibilities that could help boost the popularity of various Web3 initiatives.

* access to certain events (NFTs)

* Collectable status (NFTs)

* Cash rewards (Staking/selling in Crypto)

* Value appreciation (NFT artwork, Crypto-assets used as an investment)

At the simplest level demand is ultimately determined by the return that a person can earn from owning the specific asset.

Make sure there's a tangible benefit in the asset's value in the long run. If there is no benefit in owning the asset, it's unlikely that the value will rise over time.

Allocation and Ownership

Another thing to investigate is how division of ownership occurs.

In whitepapers, or even the plans, you'll usually find an area called tokenomics. In these sections, you will find an outline of the distribution of tokens as well as the who owns the initiative.

The breakdown should look like the one shown in Cardstarter.

When you take a brief look, just 30% of the proceeds are guaranteed in a the public sale. When you combine the amount owned by the partnership, team or private sales, as well as advisors, you'll receive a total of 50 percent.

It's possible to think that I'm being cynical however, in my personal experience the private sale and partnership can be used to...

* Insuring influencers to promote the idea

* Maintain control and ownership of the owner

* securing "high-value" individuals that raise the value perception of the venture

This will increase the value of the game through a an open sale, creating an easy way to earn money for the project's creators.

When I look at Cards It seems like this could be risky so I'd steer clear.

In cases where the majority of ownership still remains in the hands of the original creators, they typically do not have your best interests to be in the forefront. Every action you make favor them significantly.

However, if most tokens held are for owners, then there's more chance of conserving value and being used to fulfill their function instead of just the basis for a simple rug to pull.

It was a brief and concise look at some of the most important indicators that are used to determine the project's tokenomics.

This isn't any financial advise. What I've found as commonly used indicators in both good and bad projects.

Chapter 18: Bringing it all Together

Doing this for you

Take care and exercise your best judgment.

The steps and checks I've listed in this document are easy to follow and provide answers to typical practices and patterns I've witnessed scammers employ. These aren't 100% safe.

In the case of these situations, when the new security measures are implemented, the criminal subculture will always have an alternative. They'll never stop pushing the boundaries and searching for vulnerabilities.

If you are a Web3 user, Web3 area, you need to be extremely careful. It is essential to verify twice, verify, and confirm all possible ways to decrease your risk of losing money to fraudsters.

The most effective weapon you can have in your arsenal for security is common sense.

This is how I would recommend you use the tips in this guide.

1. Protect your arse

First thing to take care of is covering up the arse of your own.

You must ensure that your assets are secured as is possible. This doesn't mean you can't put your trust in exchanges, trading platforms as well as auction websites.

It is my opinion that you should not just blindly believe them.

The company's success is dependent on maintaining your customers satisfied So they'll take every step to minimize the risk of hacks and scams. As mentioned earlier that with every new initiative they introduce the market, they're attracting thousands of individuals looking for a basic attack.

It is impossible to guarantee that anything will be safe. There's always a flaw, loophole or flaw that could be exploited.

In addition, by taking precautions, like utilizing the cold wallet to keep important assets, you are creating yet another obstacle for fraudsters to get over.

For as horribly insipid as this may sound, you don't need to provide a secure environment. It's just a matter of making your security so difficult that criminals will find the easiest target.

If everyone follows these steps however, it will be a huge disappointment to a number of scammers, and could - hopefully - render the profession of scamming much more trouble that it's value.

2. Making decisions you're confident with

If you're looking at the risk of a project You don't expect they to satisfy every single requirement I've discussed in this article. A small percentage of projects won't be in a position to achieve the job.

What you want is more positive check marks rather than negative ones.

After you've reviewed the project's processes, previous activities, and even the entire team, the next step is to take a decision. The most important thing to come down to is if you're confident about transferring your money to this particular project and the group who are behind the project.

If, after doing your homework, you are left with doubts it, maybe you'll find an solution.

There is no one who can inform you (or can inform you) what projects you ought to consider backing. It's your decision to make. After completing the above tests, you'll be better positioned to make an educated decision.

There will be one or two mistakes We all make mistakes and that's the way of life. However, these tests should ensure you make better decisions.

Chapter 19: The recommended tools

Make sure you have these essential tools

It will make the process of identifying frauds simpler

If you're serious about examining websites for potential scams it is essential to have the appropriate equipment in your arsenal.

Below is a brief list of tools available in the Web3 space to aid in identifying and analysing web3 projects.

Use the method with this brief guide, with the help of the below tools.

And if you want a little more information on the tools and services I mention, head to https://DecentReviews.co and search for the specific tool you're looking at.

If we've added the application/tool to our site there's...

This is our impartial and basic details on the tool as well as the business

Real-time reviews written by everyday people just like you.

* A single star rating is based upon those reviews

It should assist you in making an informed choice. If you're looking for a tool or platform we haven't yet added, feel free to shoot an email to support@DecentReviews.co with the information and we'll add it to our list.

Then, let's get to the equipment.

Research on the community

It is an extremely easy set of tools that are available to everyone at costs.

All you really need are a few social media accounts, and accounts with a few simple communication/messaging services.

This is a quick overview of why I'd advise you to join to find out what other members are talking about.

Below isn't an exhaustive list but will be sufficient to cover 90% of chats as well as mentions of any Web3 initiative at the time at the time of writing.

Social media

Join the following social media networks to discover what people in the public and prominent personalities in the industry have to say about various projects.

* Twitter.com - This is where the bulk of Web3 users are on social media. Sign up for an account and begin search for your project. investigating.

* Facebook.com - Facebook isn't the most suitable platform option for Web3 initiatives, but there are plenty of groups to assist you in identifying and learn more about what's happening within this space.

We're a shameless Facebook group here: bit.ly/3KCB5ET

* TikTok.com - There is plenty of activity there on TikTok currently. A lot of influencers utilize TikTok to promote their own initiatives, which makes it an excellent research platform.

* YouTube Although it is not a exclusively social media there are numerous groups and influential people using the platform to discuss and sharing various ideas.

Community communications and messaging services

The most successful initiatives make use of messages and other community-based services to keep the public engaged as well as to update holders and prospective holders of any new developments.

Joining the following will permit you to join no-cost, private communities that are to get better knowledge.

* Discord.com - Discord is the most popular communication platform used for projects. A Discord account makes the process of signing

up to different chats in the community simple and quick.

* Telegram.org - Telegram is a messaging service that numerous projects utilize to inform groups of the latest advancements.

* Slack.com - Slack isn't as popular like Discord using Web3 projects however it's still worth maintaining your account just to be prepared in the event that you discover projects that use it.

NFT marketplaces

If you're thinking of purchasing an NFT one, then you'll need to make use of one of the many NFT marketplaces. We have a frequently updated list on DecentReviews.co at the following page - DecentReviews.co/category/nft-marketplaces.

These sisters will see important NFT-related details such as...

* The history of the costs of NFTs within the collection

* The past owners of each NFT in the collection

* The cost of the floor for the collection.

* Links to collection's marketing channels, as well as to the website

There are many market segments that are niche, listed below are the three largest that cover most people's requirements.

* OpenSea is the most important NFT market

* "LooksRare" is a great competitor NFT marketplace, which rewards its users

* Lootex is a market for gaming-specific NFT

Crypto exchanges

If you're considering trading in cryptocurrency, you'll require an exchange platform to help facilitate trading. There's a variety of diverse platforms to choose from.

There are several that can fulfill your expectations.

If you're looking to trade smaller currencies and you're taking the complete DeFi strategy and are using techniques such as staking to generate an income stream, you'll require additional exchanges that are more specifically designed for you.

Three exchanges are listed below that will satisfy the requirements for the vast majority of consumers. I've also tried to provide three exchanges that offer security against theft from third entities. One recommendation that does not have this is UniSwap (at at the date of this the writing).

You can read the full list of our reviewed Crypto Exchanges here - DecentReviews.co/category/crypto-exchanges

* Binance The largest and most trusted Crypto exchange

* Coinbase A different well-known exchange

* UniSwap is a great option for acquiring smaller alt-coins

Checks on the value of cryptocurrency

If you're looking at influencers and their currencies be sure to verify what the price of the assets they're advertising.

In order to do this for that, you'll have to make use of one of these options to see how the worth of the currency has fluctuated throughout time. Create a parallel between the date when the influencer did their advertisement, and then you'll determine whether they're planning the simple dump and pump.

You can find a full list of these research tools here - DecentReviews.co/category/web3-research-tools.

* Trading View is not a specific crypto platform, as it also follows traditional stock market data. However. This is the only service I've seen that has a wide range of the latest alt-coins, making their research effortless.

* CoinGecko A good alternative to determine the value of various coins within the market.

* CoinMarketCap The CoinMarketCap is the Crypto market's leading service.

Chapter 20: What is Bitcoin?

Let's first explore what bitcoin means and then begin by giving a brief background on bitcoin. Satoshi Nakamoto first published his Bitcoin white paper in 2008, and 2009 was

the year that saw its first application.

The term "Bitcoin" refers to Bitcoin is a type of digital number that is created through a mathematical operation known as"HASH" "HASH". It can be accessed using two keys: a "public" and a "private" key. One of the reasons for its most attention was the fact that it's not centralized. The ledger is stored in a chain of blocks that is the digital ledger. The ledger isn't stored in one place however, it is spread across numerous.

The source is Satoshi Nakamoto's Bitcoin whitepaper

Nakamoto was interviewed about

Evidence of Work: A random node on the network chooses the block that will be added.

Others nodes decide to choose to reject or accept this block. Validity of transactions (unspent or not signed) is a factor

Incentive programs for proof of employment Rewarding work with a block, or transactions fees.

Possible forking: Only blocks of the chain with the longest length are generally accepted by the majority. generally

In the ledger, you are able to only create a new transaction. The existing line of transactions can't be altered or modified. To comprehend this structure of data, take a look at the diagram below. This diagram is taken an original work by Satoshi Nakamoto.

Each user gets the private and public key. The keys are created by an algorithm. They are linked. If we use an open key, it will produce a unique private key. It is essential that the sure shares the public key, which may be visible to every user and helps with verification and gives a feeling of being part of.

These days, the keys are in sync, meaning that the public key that has more visibility when contrasted to private keys, could provide clues about private keys to those looking for access to the private key. In addition, more information on the user of the private key could cause concern for the person who holds the key.

Satoshi Nakamoto, who decided to remain anonymous due to reasons that are not known, created cryptocurrency, a type of cryptocurrency. What made people to choose it was that it was not managed by a single source. In the end, it removed the influence that anyone could have enjoyed if it had been under the control of a single source.

Source: Marco Canini

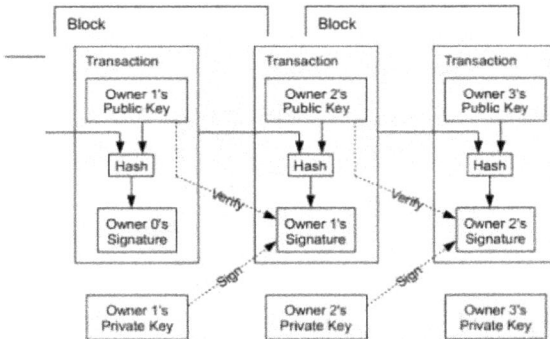

Nakamoto's Blockchain

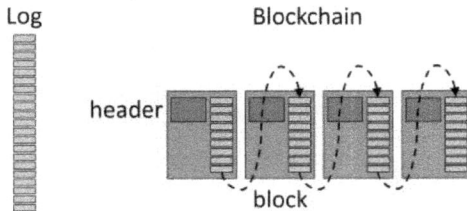

The popularity of bitcoin naturally attracted others to the marketplace who developed their own digital currencies. Therefore, a variety of alt coins came into existence. There are now well over "alternate" coins to Bitcoin. Most of them are merely duplicates. They just alter some things like the coin supply or hashing functions, or the like. Notable Altcoins are Ripple and Litecoin.

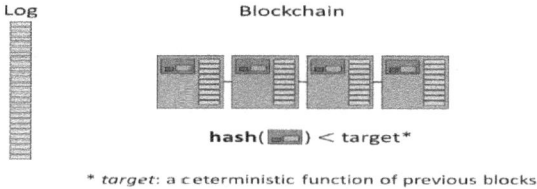

Blockchain

hash(▨) < target*

* *target*: a deterministic function of previous blocks

Phishing frauds

Phishing is the method of getting sensitive and private information such as usernames or passwords by hiding websites and other. People are tricked into believing that they have entered the data through a trusted site or on a website that has been sent to them via email or Google advertisements. The result is that the people receive an email with an impression that something is wrong with the account or their wallet, and they must rectify the situation by clicking the hyperlink. It will lead to a fake web page which is mostly similar to the official website, that has the same style as well as color schemes and fonts that make the users to believe they're in the right spot.

After the user has entered the details, they are given to the scammers which then utilize it in as they wish. They may use the information immediately or save it to use later, based on the potential upside.

Myetherwallet is the most prominent example of this kind of fraud. A fake website was developed in the exact style and appearance that the official one which prompted users provide their details as they did in the official platform. The result was huge loss to users.

The thought that the fake Myetherwallet application was among the top three applications on the App Store is frightening. How quickly it spread, and affected so many people is a sign of how vulnerable this business could be due to being vulnerable to attack users could be.

Another approach is that of airdrops. This is when fraudulent companies who claim to be genuine ones and offer vouchers for free to a huge variety of users. In addition, they require you to install an app or portal designed by those who want to make money on your behalf. Users are required to input the username and password which expose the private as well as the public keys, as this allows for the depletion of accounts.

What can you do to stay away from being victimized?

It is now time to consider what should be done in order to stop the occurrences. Answer: keep yourself aware. Stay up-to-date. The more we are aware of current events around the globe more we know about it.

Read news articles and subscribe to as much as you can. Be up to date. Talk to people you know about the topic and speak about the subject. This requires some effort from you. You must be curious. Learn more.

Some of the important things to bear in mind are the following:

Be sure that the URL that you're using when you are in this situation will be the one you see every time. Most of the time, minor differences go unnoticed or are difficult to spot. It's your hard-earned money you are dealing with in this case. Therefore, you must ensure that you are careful each occasion you're required to fill in your information. Make sure you verify your addresses.

Take a look at your gut When a website doesn't look or feel good, there is something different or there's something different from normal. STOP! Don't proceed without checking! Contact a person who is knowledgeable something or two. Make a plan! Don't just go with the flow.

A different tactic that these sites that are a bit shady employ the notion of urgency. They issue warnings. They make use of deadlines. They require the user to perform an action as fast as is possible by using big, large red titles that have the word "HURRY" flashing like a traffic signal, causing fear and anxiety in our minds. It forces users to make a decision without pondering the consequences and 99 out of 100, the outcome of which is disastrous.

Always use a secure password.

Most importantly, remember that password. It's quite common for users forget their passwords and cannot open their wallets.

Then, we'll provide a detailed explanation of how to stay away from scams as well as what are the Dos and Don'ts

Chapter 21: Mining Scams

Mining scams are a different intriguing aspect of frauds. Cloud mining is the method used by scammers. There is no doubt that cloud mining is fraudulent. Certain cloud mining companies use it for legitimate reasons. But, like every other time there are those that use cloud mining in a negative way and have used intricate schemes to swindle individuals.

Cloud mining refers to the method that involves mining bitcoins using cloud. These are the companies that permit users open accounts for them. In return, they allow users to participate in the mining process. The mining process happens in a cloud environment, thus getting rid of the costs associated with maintenance of equipment and energy.

There are companies operating with a legitimate business model as well as people who are an integral part of them. However, at the same time there are some companies who are completely off the mark with regards to the ethical and legal boundaries. The returns are one method to look at these businesses to determine if they're going to hurt you or not. If the returns are positive, there's an opportunity that it's all fine and you don't have anything to fret about. If there's no or only minimal returns, it's a red alert. Beware of these setups. They're not meant intended for the people you. or anyone else in fact.

Are the arrangements allowing unrestricted examination of the manner in which they function, what equipment they employ and how they intending to move their business to the next level? If not, you can be sure there's something they don't want the public or any other person who is not part of the circle of friends to be aware. Transparency is a must. Everyone has the right to have all the information about the business they plan to interact with. There shouldn't be any doubt about this.

Malware Scams

A malware portal serves to attack your computer and is able to strike exactly where it is required to enter your system. The malware is developed. Once the computer has been infected and the virus is in control, it takes over and is able to operate and steal personal information or files as it was intended to.

There are many ways by how the job could be accomplished.

A good example of this is when it could affect the security of your BTC wallet. If you try to transfer money to someone who is in need, your account you originally used could be altered along with a fake account belonging to a scammer.

A malware-related scam that which was noticed as"the crypto Currency Clipboard Hijackers. They employed the Windows clipboard to launch their attacks. These fraudsters used the clipboard in Windows to watch some thousand addresses for cyrptocurrency however this scam was quite huge. The one reported by major news sites was used to track 2.3 million address.

They employ the copy paste feature of the Windows system. Since addresses are typically lengthy and hard to recall When users were able the copy-paste feature to paste addresses, the fraudsters would substitute their addresses with fake addresses. They would then transfer the funds in the in the wrong people's.

This is how you can spot the kind of activity.

Your PC is slowing down and signs indicate that it's the computer slowing down

Pop ads are, well they appear, however there are too many at a point where they start to be annoying

It is possible that you'll notice an strange behavior you're not at fault for.

Fake Wallets

Scam	Lifetime		Payout to scammer	
	Days	Alive?	BTC	USD
Scam wallets	535	yes	4 105	$359 902
Scam exchanges				
BTC Promo	98	yes	44	$22 112
btcQuick		no	929	$73 218
CoinOpend	29	no	575	$264 466
Ubitex	91	no	30	$96[16]
Mining scams	Data Source			
Labcoin	Blockchain		241	$48 562
AMC	BitFunder		18 041	$1 327 590
Ice Drill	BitFunder		14 426	$1 558 008
Asic Mining	Blockchain		12.6	$5 532
Dragon Miner	Blockchain		1.63	$1 019

The fake wallets also are the favorite among scammers. They design a fake wallet in order to make people reveal the passwords and their keys. Bitcoin gold was a new product on the market, and people trying to claim a stake were presented with the fake website that was going through the domain that was "mybtgwallet.com". It was believed to be the real issue, users gave their details concerning the details of their confidential keys. Then, they were stripped of million of dollars due to the.

The scam has emptied pockets of people and incurred the victims with an amount in excess of $3.5 million

Chapter 22: The platform was recently created

You don't see "Https". Instead, there's "Http"(meaning the connection isn't secured)

ICO SCAMS

ICO refers to the term used to describe an Initial coin offering, which the creators or developers conduct in order to fundraise money to fund their business or a company or the. The primary reason for companies for conducting ICOs is to increase money and funds, the motivation of the money raising is vital. There are times when it is different. Certain groups run ICOs, and they're very serious about what they will use the money.

As that the money is raised and there's no governing agency to monitor on what the creators decide to do with the money They are totally at liberty to choose which actions to take and what not. The creators can disappear into an empty sky and disappear with the money or take it in opposite direction and operate within the lawful boundaries.

An investigation conducted in the Wall Street Journal states that one in five Initial Coin Offerings ICOshow evidence of fake activations. That's 18.6%. It's an enormous portion of the overall ICOs and had an impact on the marketplace. Someone, somewhere, was connected and in some manner with these ICOs.

The purpose of ICOs is in order to avoid the lengthy procedure of obtaining capital via banks or capital markets such as VC capitalism. The market is experiencing a huge increase in the amount of money collected by ICOs throughout the year of 2018. The initial five months of 2018 surpassed the amount raised by the previous year's total..

The trend suggests that the greater the size of this sector of the cryptocurrency world increases, the chance of it being affected by scammers and fraudsters will likely to increase.

An excellent example of an ICO fraud can be seen in The Giza Scam. Nearly $2 million was stolen.

The project was a sign of concerns when the primary provider, that was supposed to design their gadget and was notified that it had severed connections with Giza with factors that were alarming people watching. The company claimed that the program appeared to be fraudulent. They also said that they were not cooperating anymore.

The company that supplies the product, The Third Pin The Third Pin, whose CEO is Ivan Larionov announced on a Bit Coin forum that the company had taken the decision to break ties with Giza. The reason was as straightforward as the Giza Honcho who is who is known by the name of Marco Fike, was unable to communicate clearly throughout the discussions, which was a signal of trouble. In referring to a specific point in the procedure, he stated that in the event of being asked when the devices were supposed to be released, Marco Fike, failed to articulate what he was planning to achieve and the plan he had in mind. This clearly showed that the idea suggested in public wasn't properly developed since the intent wasn't clear in any way. There was no seriousness or genuineness behind the whole scheme.

This is when Giza's sole supplier made the decision to quit Giza. This was only the initial attack in the series of.

The accounts started to dwindle. The funds were transferred to different accounts.

Pump and Dump Scam

Scams involving pump and dump rely on fraudulent projection and show the potential and promise of the otherwise defunct organization. It happens on a massive size. The scammers trick purchasers to make a purchase and once prices reach a critical level, projectors will sell the digital currency and then the market around the coins would crash. The reason for this is that the opportunity wasn't present at all. The entity was dead.

The scams of pump and dump within the world of cyrptocurrency are akin. Investors, many of who aren't even ready to make a purchase, are shown promising prospects and then manipulated to believe that one day a significant player will invest in or collaborate with the entity proposed and then they're enticed to invest with a shaky prospect. The fervor created by faith-based investors then increases the cost to an extent after which the price is at its peak, which means that it is no longer able to go on and is determined when examining the quantity which was calculated by the scammers, the deflation begins. Then, in only a couple of minutes the price drops, and it's shorter-lived as you would expect.

The reason for this is an extremely simple motive. Offloading! Markets are manipulated so as to limit the risk of offloading. Not just to minimize losses, most instances, a profit is made at the expense of individuals who are left with the option of grieving. The worst part is that those who suffer realize they've taken part in the illegal act without being aware. Their actions and power of purchase led to the price going higher, and once it did then it crashed down without warning. It was too late to take a choice or exit. Once the reality sets in the moment it's over. This scenario could unfold in just a few minutes. In contrast to weeks or days.

Ponzi Schemes

The scams described above are precisely what they sound like. Everyone has heard about how Ponz operates. This scam is employed by old-fashioned criminals who are unable to come up with enough of their clever strategies. They quickly swept into the cryptocurrency market and put the entire world on the alert.

Ponzi schemes will take money from you and promise that they will multiply it. This often happens by requesting for referrals from colleagues or your family. In the second phase, you will be able to bring an amount of capital that is used to repay the riches of those who first. Investors who are newer not always successful when it comes to wealth returning, and multiplied, because after that the scheme was ended due to fraud and fraud. Did I mention the fact that investing takes place on a non-existent organization? That means that there wasn't a way to increase wealth, other than taking money from investors who were referred to them by you?

Chapter 23: It sounds nice and cozy!

The schemes are in operation for indefinitely as long as the cat hasn't left the bag. When investors figure out they've been investing into a real estate an item that isn't available everywhere in the world the first step is to seek a reward. This obviously doesn't go smoothly? In the present, it's way too late. The majority of money is being transported into foreign countries, deposited or employed to finance illegal actions, and it could be anyplace on the planet. The issue is not what the location of the money is located or how it has utilized, the most important thing is that by the time it's gone, individuals were swindled. The severity of the harm caused can be quantified, but the impact it caused isn't.

The Signs to Look for the Signs of a Ponzi fraud

The earnings are astronomically high.

The company's success depends on the referrals

The model of business feels a bit sloppy

Incomplete transparency and a lack in information about the company as well as the people who run it

They are typically easily found. When you are able to look them up with an eye for clues, some exertion, it could uncover a scam prior to it's way too far.

Real Life scams examples

This is a complete list of scams that are real. You can be sure that learning about these scams might make you nervous and you may be dissuaded to join the scam if you had a strategy at all to take part in the scam. However, remember that this ebook provides an understanding of what it is as well as the time and date of when and the reason for it, and the consequences. I was forced to switch between two options and then decide whether or not to include them in the article. Due to the sheer number of frauds and scams, certain of them are massive in terms of volume, and also the extent of destruction they have left on their wake. All the bad news related to one incident which has occurred within the same location can make doubts appear in the mind of potential investors. There is a proven fact that if someone is exposed to warnings that are sporadic from various sources, it has the most solid and greater positive impact in that the person doesn't get scared. They absorb the info each one at a time and help to maintain the speed of mind. This means that the process of decision-making also happens with a calming and efficient rate. This is a type an approach to slow penetration. If an article, or ebook in this instance chooses to place everything into one place this could have the result of panic, chaos and even paranoia. Be assured that this ebook is solely intended to inform readers. It is possible that there are some who are making plans for the moment to leap, and then there is those who are past the point of preparing and waiting for that final push to get them to take that leap I'm sure this ebook is available on their computers, laptops, or tablets at the right the right time. To ensure that prior to taking the plunge to take a review of this book and determine whether they are adequately preparing themselves for the wild and unpredictable world of cryptocurrency currency.

Where do we go?

Plexcoin

Dominic Lacroix, the founder of Plexcoin was sentenced to prison for executing the fraudulent ICO which raised more than $15 million from thousands investors. Lacroix and his activities attracted the attention of regulators prior to the ICO was deemed illegal, was told to stop the campaign. The founder decided to proceed and not pay any to. The rash decision earned him charges of contempt of court and a jail sentence. In addition the company he runs DL Innov were slapped with an $110,000 fine.

He was in the ccurtroom and was requested to pay the money. In response to the request, he obliged.

Bitconnect

Divyesh Darji who was alleged to be among those responsible for the Bitconnect fraud was taken into custody in Dubai in the year 2000. It was claimed that Bitconnect took away around 15 million dollars from investors is enough to prompt the Gujarat Criminal Investigation Department (CID) to initiate the process.

The business was incorporated with the UK and was locatec in Surat. They launched a campaign to promote their business through social media, and also organized parties throughout all over the world, and received the attention they wanted. The slogan read "60% monthly nterest" which was pretty appealing for all the investors who were willing to invest. In the peak of its popularity, the value for BCC was $363.62 which is now at $0.67. The company was closed due to bad media as well as US regulation as the reason.

OneCoin

OneCoin was officially identified as the official name of a Ponzi scheme operating in India. It claimed to have been licensed in Vietnam but Vietnam has since denied the allegations. Numerous scandals around the globe across different nations proved OneCoin certainly was not a fraud.

Thailand, Croatia, Bulgaria, Finland and Norway warned that investors of the possibility dangers that could be posed by the company.

In 2016, nearly 30 million dollars were confiscated in 2016 by the Chinese government after they made the decision to investigate the situation.

CentraTech

CentraTech CentraTech HTML0 is a different name on the list of frauds. The company's founders raised nearly $32 million from an ICO that was held last year. What makes it on the list this year is due to the huge name of popular culture are included such including Floyd Mayweather and DJ Khaled. It was crucial to highlight this case due to the high-profile nature of the hype around it. The marketing took over and added A-liters for bid. This was the first time for a cryptocurrency. It was evident that the fame and trustworthiness were accompanied by name recognition. The coattails ride was an easy but highly successful strategy, which resulted as a huge amount of cash arriving.

Persuading investors to invest is one of the main targets of every business, and if you have big names to their backs, most of the work was accomplished.

The amount of money involved of the fraud seems somewhat less when we consider the ease of doing it for them to pull off. However, we may not know the reason what they did to get the level they could have.

The team could be contemplating a 65-year sentence in prison.

The list includes cryptocurrency currencies that are blacklisted.

Below is a short overview of the cryptocurrency currencies that have been banned or are on the verge of being to being among the numerous.

Below is a listing of names much more likely fraudulent Ponzi schemes rather than real organizations

BCC Cash (note that this is distinct in comparison to Bitcoin Cash)

BCHconnect

Billion Bit Club

Binary Coin

Bit Sequence

BitAI

Bitchamps

Bitclub/clubcoin

Bitcoin Ascension (pyramid scheme)

Bitconnect X

Bitether

Bitfinite

Bitfintech

Bitglare Coin

Btchash

Btc-Rush

Btcwait

Chrysos

Coinrium

Cointeum

Coinspace

Dascoin

Ecomcash

Eigencoin

ETHconnect

Etherbanking

Exacoin

Falcon Coin

Farstcoin

Ficoin

Firstcoin

Forzacoin

Futurecoin

FUU Coin

Gold Reward Token

Goldgate

Hedgeconnect

Hextracoin

Home Block Coin

HotCrypto

Hydrocoin

Ibiscoin

iCenter

Ideacoin

IFan

Iotaconnect

Knox Coin

Legendcoin

Lendconnect

Lendera

Libra Coin

Liteconnect

Loancoin

Martcoin

Moneroconnect

Monetize Coin

Monyx

Neoconnect

Numiv

Oalend Coin

Onecoin

Pagarex

Purpose/DUBI

Regalcoin

Rothscoin

Secular Coin

SFICoin

Steneum

Stepium (pyramid scheme)

Swisscoin (pyramid scheme)

Tenocoin

TEX Coin

Thorn Coin

Ucoin Cash

Unix Coin

USI Tech

WCI

Western Coin

XRPconnect

Defunct ponzi schemes:

Ambis

Bitcoinly

Bitconnect

Bithaul

Bitlake

Bitpetite

Bitsupreme

Btcbox.cc

Chain.Group

Coinreum

Control Finance

Cryptodouble

Davor

Ethtrade

Laser Online

LoopX

Mavro

Mecoin

Metizer

Microhash

Paycoin

Plexcoin

Thunderbit

Vixice

Vone

What can you do to stay clear of these scams

There are always warning signs. They are sometimes too visible to be noticed, and other times they're not. Yet, shockingly, the warning signs that are obvious don't do enough to stop people. If you're a casual investor who's not looking to stay for the long run or are simply following some trend or do this out of curiosity, become prey. The businesses that have those not-so-glaring flaws can also make money and target the smarter of an average investor. It seems that every scammer is a victim for their own. The idea of scamming even if it's not so common within the crypto currency industry, is easy. It's also true to a certain degree. Since as the those who don't invest the time and effort to learn as much as they can about fraudulent schemes, there'll be a person who can profit from this kind of behavior.

Chapter 24: Public Profile

If creators have promised the public a repository, then there must exist one. There is no alternative. With no front, or an appearance that appears authentic, there's no assurance that the organization or team is actually in existence. It is not clear if there is a strategy for the future, and there's no assurance that they have an engineering team that is who are working on the product. This could be all eyewash and there's nothing better to prove contrary than to witness it.

Zero Activity

If there's no activity over longer periods of time It indicates something's incorrect. The majority of Crypto currencies is launched and begins with the hope that they will grow exponentially. It's all created through marketing or referrals and broad statements. However, the hype fades away. It's because they lack the endurance or perseverance to carry on. In the end that the absence of any activity begins to appear. It is a huge indicator that the outlook is dark and being part of the process will never be worth the effort. It's virtually impossible for companies to restart and rise after having fizzled out, public has heard about it and the company is not impression among shareholders. Therefore, a business that's in a downward spiral, slowing completely halted, never is it ever able to get back on track. It is important to be wary of such businesses.[]

Smaller group

The general consensus is that in order in order for something to succeed an enthusiastic group of people, who work together professionally will be required. An individual show eventually, will end up crashing as the popularity rises. Therefore, the larger the group more impressive, it indicates that the business has established the roles of certain people. This also shows that this company will remain for the long term.

No advisors

Advisors can be a valuable contribution to the firm. They help keep the company in the right direction when things get rough. The ones who have to deal with every day work in times of being down and out, it's the time that advisors come in and guide the boat to the right direction. Therefore, the presence of one or more advisors confirms commitment and demonstrates commitment to the cause.

No diversity

In the past A large group has higher chances of succeeding over a smaller one. In practical terms! Once the roles have been clarified, and there's one person who can do the work, the process is simple and easy. Simply a bunch of tech geeks will not suffice. The company requires people who have different skills to grow. Engineers, marketers, designers and coordinators are equally essential if the business wants to for a big growth.

Team Anonymous

In the past, anonymity was an issue of admiration in the world of cryptocurrency. The public was used to behaving according to a specific way. This could be because the man who created Bit coin who has a value of $700 million, chose not to be anonymous until today. However, that was back in the day. The industry has exploded in size and is now something of a gigantic scale and is now a source of the possibility of suspicion. This industry must gets to act like a mature business. The situation must be changed. Could we envis on a scenario where the chief executive of Ford motors is able to choose not be noticed by any one and is buried in the darkness? No! The industry develops, and it's evolving quite nicely. The industry must function like every other industry and have people who a'e social media profiles and presence

No team engagement

The team must be able interact with the community they've made the decision to be a part of. It's a positive way to make everybody believe they're staying and do not have anything to hide from the outside world. Think about the next neighbor you live with has a mysterious personality and isn't talking to anybody in the street. Although he may be an honest person, they speak in quiet tones and are convinced that there's something troubling him even though there's nothing to worry about.

Infighting that is exposed

The team may not be cohesive, it is evident. It can happen and is viewed in people in the spotlight. This indicates that the time for closure is fast approaching. The negative publicity that comes with it is something is difficult to recover from. Imagine the reverse, everyone taking selfies and making pictures while on vacation. What would be the best thing that you could see and create feelings of warmth to anyone who is watching? Would fighting be the preferred option?